SURVIVAL KIT
FIVE KEYS TO
SPIRITUAL GROWTH

Ralph W. Neighbour Jr. and Bill Latham

Lifeway™ press

Brentwood, Tennessee

© 1996 Lifeway Press® • Originally published 1979 • Revised 1996, 2019
Reprinted October 2023

No part of this book may be reproduced or transmitted in any form or by any means, electronic or mechanical, including photocopying and recording, or by any information storage or retrieval system, except as may be expressly permitted in writing by the publisher. Requests for permission should be addressed in writing to Lifeway Press®; 200 Powell Place, Suite 100; Brentwood, TN 37027-7707.

ISBN 978-1-5359-6837-9 • Item 005817330

Dewey decimal classification: 248.4 • Subject headings: CHRISTIAN LIFE \ SALVATION

Unless indicated otherwise, Scripture quotations are taken from the Christian Standard Bible®, Copyright © 2017 by Holman Bible Publishers. Used by permission. Christian Standard Bible® and CSB® are federally registered trademarks of Holman Bible Publishers. Scripture quotations marked ESV are taken from the ESV® Bible (The Holy Bible, English Standard Version®), copyright © 2001 by Crossway, a publishing ministry of Good News Publishers. Used by permission. All rights reserved. Scripture quotations marked NIV are taken from the Holy Bible, New International Version®, NIV®. Copyright © 1973, 1978, 1984, 2011 by Biblica, Inc.™ Used by permission of Zondervan. All rights reserved worldwide. www.zondervan.com. The "NIV" and "New International Version" are trademarks registered in the United States Patent and Trademark Office by Biblica, Inc.™ Scripture quotations marked GNT are taken from the Good News Translation in Today's English Version, Second Edition. Copyright © 1992 by American Bible Society. Used by permission. Scripture quotations marked KJV are taken from the Holy Bible, King James Version.

To order additional copies of this resource, write to Lifeway Resources Customer Service; 200 Powell Place, Suite 100; Brentwood, TN 37027-7707; fax order to 615-251-5933; phone toll free 800-458-2772; email orderentry@lifeway.com; or order online at Lifeway.com.

Printed in the United States of America

Groups Ministry Publishing • Lifeway Resources • 200 Powell Place, Suite 100 • Brentwood, TN 37027-7707

CONTENTS

INTRODUCTION

WARNING: Being a Christian Is Far More than Trusting Christ for Salvation

When you read that warning, your reaction was probably something like "Tell me something new. I found that out within twenty-four hours of becoming a Christian!" You've probably also discovered that the harder you try, the more difficult it becomes to grow spiritually and to live your faith. Each day when you walk out to face the world, you put everything but the security of your salvation on the line. Satan will stop at nothing to keep you from growing, serving, ministering, and witnessing effectively. He wants to rob you of your fellowship with the Father and to paralyze your life as a disciple. But take heart! Survival is more than just the name of the game. It's a promised certainty for you if you want it.

Shortly before Jesus died on the cross, He prayed the most intense prayer recorded in the Bible. Are you ready for this? That prayer was for you. Jesus must have wanted you to know what He said because He left a record of it for you in John 17.

> Get your Bible now and read in John 17 what Jesus said to God about you and what He asked God to do for you.

> Now let's change what Jesus said to the present tense and make it as personal as possible for you. Place your name in each blank on the following page and allow yourself to feel the awe and wonder of Jesus the Savior talking to God the Father about you.

I pray for _____. I am not praying for the world but

for _____ you have given me, for _____ [is] yours.

Everything I have is yours, and everything you have is mine, and

I am glorified in _____. Now I am coming to you, and I

speak these things in the world so that _____ may have my

joy completed in [him or her]. I have given _____ your word.

The world hated _____ because _____ [is] not of the

world, just as I am not of the world. I am not praying that you take

_____ out of the world but that you protect _____ from

the evil one. _____ [is] not of the world, just as I am not of the

world. Sanctify _____ by the truth; your word is truth. As you

sent me into the world, I also have sent _____ into the world.

I sanctify myself for _____, so that _____ also may

be sanctified by the truth. Righteous Father, the world has not known

you. However, I have known you, and _____ [has] known

that you sent me. I made your name known to _____ and

will continue to make it known, so that the love you have loved

me with may be in _____ and I may be in _____.

JOHN 17:9-10,13-19,25-26

SURVIVAL KIT

You can have fellowship with the Father that grows deeper each day. You can grow spiritually and live victoriously. God wants this for you, Christ died to make it possible, and the power of the Holy Spirit is yours to enable you to have it.

First of all, you should set apart a definite time and place to meet your Lord daily. Call it your quiet time. As much as possible, you should plan to meet Him at the same place and time each day.

Decide now when you'll have your daily quiet time and record the time and place.

For the next six weeks, use the daily activities in this book as a guide for your quiet time. Do only one day's work at a time. Your goal is to develop and strengthen new habits in your life, and that will take time. Having a daily quiet time is as important to your survival as anything else you'll do.

As you grow spiritually, you'll learn many truths. The five you'll learn about in this Bible study are critical to your survival. Your hand can help you remember these truths.

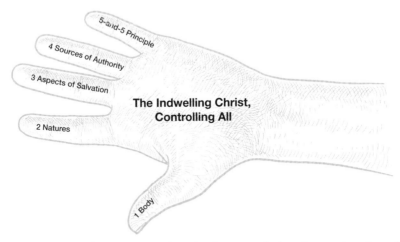

Notice the way the truths are arranged on the drawing of a hand. Your thumb works with each of the other fingers. Being part of the body of Christ is important to the other truths. Survival depends on your combining the first truth with the others.

Note that "The Indwelling Christ, Controlling All" is central. For your survival, the beginning point and the power to continue growing rest in Christ's lordship over your life.

Charting Your Course for Survival

You already know from experience that being a Christian isn't easy. Satan will stop at nothing to defeat your efforts to grow and serve your new Master. And that's scary! But Christ wants you to know that just as surely as He has saved you and will keep you saved, He can give you victory over everything Satan can throw at you.

You can be a survivor in your Christian life!

As you work through *Survival Kit,* you'll learn how to tackle key challenges that are critical to your survival as a Christian. Each week you'll learn about one of the truths on the hand drawing, and you'll see how that truth relates to a key challenge you'll face in your daily walk with Christ.

FOUNDATION WEEK

KEY TRUTH: The Indwelling Christ, Controlling All
KEY DANGER: Having a life without an adequate foundation for Christian growth
KEY CHALLENGE: Developing habits, attitudes, and commitments that ensure Christian growth

The foundation on which your survival depends is your relationship with Christ, who dwells in you. The best way to establish and strengthen that foundation is to spend quality time alone with Him in Bible study, prayer, and meditation. These habits will help you keep Christ at the center of your life.

WEEK 1

KEY TRUTH: One Body: Its Life and Service
KEY DANGER: Being a lone-ranger Christian
KEY CHALLENGE: Learning to live in a new relationship

Every Christian needs to learn to live in a new relationship with other Christians. The Bible teaches that all believers make up the body of Christ, and a church is the local expression of His body. The place where spiritual growth is easiest and most natural is in the body—the fellowship of believers who make up a local church. As you study about one body, you'll learn that continuing growth in your life as a Christian strongly depends on your relationship to the body of Christ.

WEEK 2

KEY TRUTH: Two Natures: Old and New
KEY DANGER: Being overconfident or trying to fake the Christian life
KEY CHALLENGE: Learning to address your inner conflict with sin

Every Christian soon learns that even though the victory is real, life isn't always smooth. All the struggles over which you thought you had victory keep trying to creep back into your life. Then you come face-to-face with the fact that the old nature didn't go away when you trusted Christ and He gave you a new nature. The old nature is the way Satan tries to get back into your life to defeat you and destroy your fellowship with the Father. As long as you live, the old nature will be locked in conflict with your new nature. The next critical issue you must wrestle with is your inner conflict with sin.

WEEK 3

KEY TRUTH: Three Aspects of Salvation: Beginning, Process, and Completion
KEY DANGER:: Ceasing to grow as a Christian
KEY CHALLENGE: Resolving doubts about your experience with Christ

Do you remember how quickly Satan used your old nature to try to get back into your life? Suddenly you were filled with doubts and questions: *How can this be happening? It isn't supposed to be this way! What can I do?* You're embarrassed and ashamed; you don't want to disappoint friends and relatives; and most of all, you don't want to disappoint and embarrass God.

Each time you ask yourself, *What am I going to do?* Satan gives you an option: "Fake it. Cover up all the sins that are creeping back into your life. Pretend to be all you think God and others expect you to be. Play the part like an actor on a stage."

The only problem with faking it is that you can't fool yourself. You soon realize you're living a lie. You have no inner victory. You realize Satan has defeated you, and you feel like a hypocrite. That's why it's important for you to learn to accept your inner conflict with sin as a reality and confront it. Failing to understand and address your inner conflict with sin opens the door for Satan to hit you with doubts about your experience with Christ. He'll point at the old nature that's giving you a hard time and whisper, "See that? If you were really saved, you wouldn't have those feelings or doing those things."

Survival Kit will teach you that your salvation has three aspects.

1. It's a point in time when Christ saved you from the condemnation of sin and indwelled you as your Lord.
2. It's a process in time as the power of the Holy Spirit helps your new nature gain daily victories over the power and influence of sin.
3. It's a final point in time when Christ will forever set you free from the presence of sin.

WEEK 4

KEY TRUTH: Four Sources of Authority: Inadequate and Adequate
KEY DANGER: Being sidetracked by false leaders and false causes
KEY CHALLENGE: Finding a dependable authority for discovering truth and making decisions

The fourth key issue is a big one! Until you understand your authority for discovering what's true, you'll never feel sure about how to live out your faith in the community of believers and in the world. You'll learn that three inadequate sources of authority have a certain role in determining truth. But the true, ultimate source of authority for a Christian is the written Word of God, the Bible.

WEEK 5

KEY TRUTH: The Five-and-Five Principle: Reaching Others through Prayer and Witnessing
KEY DANGER: Becoming a silent Christian
KEY CHALLENGE: Learning to share your faith effectively with lost people

Have you already met some silent Christians, who never share their faith with others? If you haven't, you will. You may wonder why they have no desire to tell others about what Christ has done for them. You need to learn how to avoid being trapped in the silent-Christian syndrome. Christians who don't verbally witness aren't sharing the gospel as effectively as they could be. Although they may be busy in church, their Christian lives will be like a fruit tree without fruit. *Survival Kit* will help you learn how to keep from becoming a silent Christian by using the Five-and-Five Principle to share your faith with others.

COURSE MAP

WEEK	KEY TRUTH	KEY DANGER	KEY CHALLENGE
Foundation Week	The Indwelling Christ, Controlling All	Having a life without an adequate foundation for Christian growth	Developing habits, attitudes, and commitments that ensure spiritual growth
Week 1	One Body: Its Life and Service	Being a lone-ranger Christian	Learning to live in a new relationship
Week 2	Two Natures: Old and New	Being overconfident or trying to fake the Christian life	Learning to address your inner conflict with sin
Week 3	Three Aspects of Salvation: Beginning, Process, and Completion	Ceasing to grow as a Christian	Resolving doubts about your experience with Christ
Week 4	Four Sources of Authority: Inadequate and Adequate	Being sidetracked by false leaders and false causes	Finding a dependable authority for discovering truth and making decisions
Week 5	The Five-and-Five Principle: Reaching Others through Prayer and Witnessing	Becoming a silent Christian	Learning to share your faith effectively with lost people

Foundation Week

THE INDWELLING CHRIST

CONTROLLING ALL

The Christian life is a marathon, not a sprint.

The Bible often refers to the Christian life as a race (see Gal. 2:2; 5:7; Phil. 2:16, 2 Tim. 4:7; Heb. 12:1). Preparing for a race requires you to invest time in core training disciplines. You want to eat right and perform exercises that will build your cardiovascular health. As you commit to a healthful diet and a regular exercise routine, your physical stamina will increase. Yet as Christians, we recognize that our spiritual health is even more important than our physical health.

Like preparing for a race, the Christian life has two core disciplines—Bible reading and prayer—aimed at strengthening our spiritual health. More than any other disciplines, these two prepare us to run the spiritual race before us.

The theme for this week is:

The Indwelling Christ, Controlling All

Believers pursue Bible reading and prayer not to fill their heads with knowledge or to check an obedience box but rather to deepen their relationship with the indwelling Christ.

How to Establish a Quiet Time

Read 1 John 4:13-16.

Would you expect to be healthy if the only time you ate a meal were on Sunday?
Of course not! You wouldn't survive long. Do you think you'll be spiritually healthy
if Sunday were the only time you nourished yourself spiritually?

A daily quiet time provides the regular, continuing spiritual nourishment you must have.
Each day you must find a time to be alone with Christ. You'll be pleased with the results.
You'll feel the joy and excitement of a healthy relationship between you and your Lord.

Look again at the hand drawing on page 6. Remember that the central part of the hand
represents "The Indwelling Christ, Controlling All." A daily quiet time is all-important
because it provides regular contact with Jesus Christ, the source of your spiritual life.

**Do an honest evaluation now. Check the statement that best describes
your quiet time.**

☐ My quiet time is a daily practice in my life, and I feel good about
it just as it is.

☐ My quiet time is a daily practice in my life, but it doesn't seem
to be as meaningful as I think it should be.

☐ My quiet times are irregular and not as meaningful as I think
they should be.

☐ I don't practice a quiet time, but I feel the need to do so.

If you checked any of the last three statements, the following guidelines will help
you establish or strengthen your own quiet time.

GUIDELINES FOR A QUIET TIME

HAVE A SPECIFIC TIME AND PLACE FOR YOUR QUIET TIME. Consider your quiet time an appointment with Christ. You need to be at a specific place at a specific time for that appointment, just as you would for an appointment with your doctor. Remember, you have an appointment with Christ. He will be waiting there for you. That reality puts your quiet time in a different light, doesn't it? Giving first priority to your quiet time is easier when you remember that Jesus is waiting for you at the appointed place and time. If possible, that time should be at the beginning of your day. Your entire day will be different if you begin it with Christ.

BE CONSISTENT. If you meet with Jesus only on a hit-or-miss basis, ask yourself whether you're really being serious about spending time alone with Him. People who work with computers use the expression "Garbage in, garbage out." Giving your computer wrong information to work with keeps it from doing what it's supposed to do. The same is true of your life in the world. A quiet time at the beginning of your day is the way you program yourself to let Christ be Lord of your life that day.

HAVE A BIBLE AND A PENCIL HANDY. Five days each week you'll need these two tools to do your work in *Survival Kit*. The other two days you should use your Bible and any other materials you use on Sunday, such as Bible-study books, to participate in opportunities your church provides to help you learn and grow spiritually. As you mature in your quiet-time practice, you'll probably want to add a journal for making notes about what you learn and experience.

BEGIN YOUR QUIET TIME WITH PRAYER. Open your heart to Christ. Affirm His right to teach, discipline, and direct you as you study and meditate. Tell Christ how much you love Him. Share your concerns with Him.

TAKE TIME TO LET CHRIST SPEAK TO YOU. Bible reading will always be the central part of your quiet time. But praying and quickly reading the Bible aren't enough. You must pause and allow Christ to speak to you as you meditate on His words.

END YOUR QUIET TIME WITH A DEFINITE COMMITMENT FOR THE DAY. Decide how you can live out what Christ has revealed to you during your quiet time. This is a practical way to extend your faith into the way you live your life.

SURVIVAL KIT

■ **Have today's quiet time right now.**

1. First pray. Express your love for God. Thank Him for giving you His life through Christ. Share with God the special ways you need His power in your life today. Ask Him to live through you as you walk in the world today.

2. Next read 1 John 4:13-16. It's quoted here from the Christian Standard Bible:

> This is how we know that we remain in him and he in us: He has given us of his Spirit. And we have seen and we testify that the Father has sent his Son as the world's Savior. Whoever confesses that Jesus is the Son of God— God remains in him and he in God. And we have come to know and to believe the love that God has for us.
>
> **1 JOHN 4:13-16**

3. Now allow God to nourish you as you meditate on what you've read. One way to digest the thoughts in a Scripture passage is to rewrite that passage in your own words. Doing this quickly lets you know whether you understand what you read. Take time now to rewrite 1 John 4:13-16 in your own words.

Another way to meditate on a passage of Scripture is to ask yourself questions about the passage. Let's do that now. Don't worry if the answers to some of the questions aren't readily apparent. These are general questions to guide your meditation. Different passages have different truths to teach you, so there may not always be an answer to every question. Also remember that God may not reveal the answers to all of your questions at this time. He may reveal only the part He wants you to know right now. Simply open your heart and trust the Holy Spirit to teach you as you look for answers.

■ **Review 1 John 4:13-16 and answer the following questions.**

Is there a truth that should influence what I believe, how I feel,
or the way I behave?

Is there an example to follow or avoid?

Is there a command to obey?

Is there a promise to claim?

As a Christian, you've personally experienced the truth that God the
Father sent Jesus Christ to be your Lord as well as your Savior. In
what ways can you obey His lordship by living out the truths He has
taught you from 1 John 4:13-16? End today's quiet time by recording
at least one specific way you'll put to work what you've learned in
your life today.

DAY 2

Using Your Bible as a Source of Christian Growth

Read Psalms 119:11,15-16; 40:8.

Your daily quiet time should always focus on Scripture. The indwelling Christ will speak to your heart as you read and meditate on the Word of God. While you work through *Survival Kit,* you should read the assigned passage at the beginning of each day's study. Then use the questions you learned yesterday to meditate on the passage.

Do you have a good study Bible? Buying one of these will be a good investment in your spiritual growth. You'll gain a better understanding of many passages if you use a modern translation. As a rule, unless otherwise noted, all Scriptures used in this book are taken from the Christian Standard Bible, a modern translation that accurately presents the Bible's original meaning in clear, readable language.

You may have a problem finding books, chapters, and verses in your Bible. That's OK. Many of your fellow Christians have the same problem. Don't hesitate to use the contents page at the front of your Bible to locate a book.

Today's verses are in the Psalms. Scan the Book of Psalms and notice the arrangement of the chapters (large numbers) and verses (small numbers). Find and read Psalm 119:11. Where did the writer say he kept the Word of God?

One way we say, "I have it memorized" is "I know it by heart." The writer of Psalm 119:11 used that same word, *heart,* to identify where he kept God's Word.

The last part of that same verse tells one great value of memorizing Scripture. What's that value? Record it here.

Memorizing God's Word can help you keep from sinning against God. Now locate and read Psalm 40:8. If you don't have a Bible nearby, where can you keep a supply of Scripture for use in any emergency?

Locate Psalm 119 and read verses 15-16. Those verses tell you something that will happen to you more fully as you develop the discipline of memorizing God's Word. Describe what will happen to you.

Isn't knowing you'll enjoy greater joy and pleasure as you memorize God's Word exciting? And you can memorize God's Word as easily as you've memorized many other details.

■ **In the list below, circle the areas in which you currently use your memory to recall needed information.**

Telephone numbers	Street names
ZIP codes	Names of people
Future dates	License numbers
Mathematical formulas	Scripture verses
Spellings of words	Passwords

No other word of advice in *Survival Kit* will have greater value for your spiritual growth than this one:

Make memorizing Scripture a regular habit.

You can easily memorize Scripture. To get started, locate the eight Scripture-memory cards printed at the back of your book. The cards are designed to be pocket-sized so that you can cut them off and refer to them as you need them. The first verse you'll learn is Psalm 119:11.

Why bother to learn the exact words of a Scripture verse? Let me suggest four reasons.

1. It's easier to recall a verse word for word than in a vaguely summarized form.
2. It's easier to meditate on a verse when you can repeat it to yourself.
3. Verses you've memorized will strengthen you and give you assurance when you're fighting temptation, telling others about Christ, and explaining what you believe.
4. Above all, the Lord of your life wants you to know His holy Word.

Can you add other benefits of memorizing Scripture?

Begin now. Cut out the verses as they're assigned in your daily studies. From now on you should memorize one new verse each week through week 3. In weeks 4 and 5 you should memorize two Scripture passages each week. Display the verses in prominent places: above the kitchen sink, on the bathroom mirror, over your workbench or desk, or near your computer. Where you display the verses isn't as important as displaying them in a place where you'll see them often. With a little planning and effort you can use brief bits of time during the day that are now idle. You can memorize while dressing, riding, exercising, waiting, resting, and so on.

Identify four places where you can display your Scripture-memory cards.

As you continue to memorize verses, regularly review all of the verses you've learned. You must reinforce your learning if you expect it to stay with you. To review, turn the cards so that you see the side with the printed reference. Say that verse out loud to yourself. Then turn the card over to see if you repeated it perfectly. If you repeated the verse perfectly, set the card aside. If you didn't repeat the verse perfectly, return it to the bottom of the stack.

Scripture is your source of authority, your guidebook as a Christian. Having Scripture available when you need it is important. And many times when you need Scripture most, you may not have a Bible.

Learn your verses as though your spiritual growth depended on it—because it does!

Are you ready to commit yourself to a pattern of regularly memorizing Scripture? If so, use your own words to write a personal note to Christ expressing your commitment to hide His Word in your heart.

Dear Jesus,

DAY 3

Learning to Pray

Read Matthew 6:9-13.

How do you feel about praying? Do you find talking to God an easy, natural thing to do? Or do you feel hesitant and awkward when you try to pray, especially when you're asked to pray aloud?

 Read the following statements and choose any that reflect what you think or feel when you try to pray.

- [ ] I'm afraid I'll say something to God that I shouldn't or ask Him for something I shouldn't.
- [ ] Often I don't know where to start or what to pray about.
- [ ] I'm afraid I'll embarrass myself because I can't pray a beautiful, fancy prayer like other people.

You don't have a problem talking to your closest friend, do you? How do you feel about talking to that friend? List some benefits and blessings of being able to talk to a close, trusted friend. Also list some feelings you have about having a friend like that.

When Jesus' followers asked Him to teach them how to pray, He gave them a model to follow. We often call that model the Lord's Prayer. Your Scripture reading for today records that prayer. If you haven't already read the passage, do so now. Find Matthew in your Bible's table of contents or try opening your Bible one fourth of the way from the back.

How did Jesus say we should address God when we pray? Record the word here.

How would you feel about talking to your father if he were not only your best friend but also the most perfect father in all the world? God is your Father—a perfect Father who dearly loves you and would do anything in the world for you that's for your good, your happiness, and your well-being. You can talk to Him freely and openly. He knows all about you and loves you just as you are. He's eager for you to talk with Him just as a child would talk with a perfect, loving, caring father. He doesn't expect you to use fancy phrases or eloquent speech. He just wants you to be you and talk to Him from your heart.

Jesus also taught His followers the kinds of topics they should pray about. These aren't all the things we'll ever want to pray about, but the list of topics is a good beginning.

The topics Jesus prayed about are listed on the left side of the following chart. Open your Bible to Matthew 6:9-13 and copy the Model Prayer on the right side of the chart, matching each phrase or sentence with one of the topics on the left. Begin with the words "Our Father."

Topics in the Model Prayer	The Model Prayer
Addressing God properly	
Showing respect for God's name	
Committing ourselves and all on earth to God's plan	
Asking God to provide for our needs (not our wants)	
Asking God for forgiveness	
Asking God for protection	
Declaring God's rule over us to be our greatest desire	
Ending our prayer properly	

Use the following outline to check your work. You should have matched each topic with all or part of the verse marked beside the topic in the outline.

- Addressing God properly (verse 9)
- Showing respect for God's name (verse 9)
- Committing ourselves and all on earth to God's plans (verse 10)
- Asking God to provide for our needs (not our wants; verse 11)
- Asking God for protection (verse 13)
- Declaring God's rule over us to be our greatest wish (verse 13)
- Ending our prayer properly (verse 13)

Does Matthew 6:9-13 seem more clear to you now that you've matched what it says with topics in the outline? You can see from this outline that any one of the topics could become a prayer all by itself. At different times you'll feel a need to pray more specifically about one of these topics than some of the others.

The best way to learn to pray is to pray.

In a moment I'm going to ask you to conclude today's study by praying. First I want you to collect your thoughts and decide what you want to talk to God about this time. Let's use the Model Prayer as a guide.

What will you say to God to show how much you respect and honor Him?

What part of your life and your world do you need to commit to God's control today?

Do you need to ask for God's forgiveness? For what?

Where do you need God's protection in your life today?

What can you say and do to recognize God's rule over your life today?

Now use the plan you've outlined to conclude your study with prayer.

Understanding What Has Happened to You

Read 2 Corinthians 5:17; Colossians 1:21-22,27.

As the quality of your daily quiet time grows deeper, you should be aware that some things are changing in your life. Second Corinthians 5:17 talks about those changes.

■ **Find 2 Corinthians 5:17 in your Bible and read it now.**

> Three key phrases in 2 Corinthians 5:17 sum up what has been happening in your life since you became a Christian. Find those key phrases and complete the sentences below.
> Your _____ way of life is passing away.
> Your _____ way of life is coming into being.
> All this is happening because …

Yes, Christ makes the difference between your old life and your new life. Colossians 1:21-22 gives the reason for these changes. Christ is now living in you and controlling you.

■ **Find and read Colossians 1:21-22 now.**

> According to Colossians 1:21, what was your attitude toward God before you became a Christian? Check any of the following that apply.
> ☐ Friendly   ☐ Alienated   ☐ Hostile
> ☐ Peaceable ☐ Harmonious ☐ Enemies

> According to Colossians 1:21, how did God view our deeds and thoughts before we became Christians? Check any of the following that apply.
> ☐ Wicked   ☐ Uninformed
> ☐ Excusable ☐ Evil

You may have thought you really weren't that bad before you became a Christian. And you may feel a little uncomfortable seeing Scripture describe your relationship with God as hostile, alienated, and enemies. You may be just as uncomfortable knowing that, in God's sight, the things you thought and did were wicked and evil. That feeling of discomfort and embarrassment is another reason to be grateful to Him for loving you and saving you in spite of what you were.

Since you became a Christian, some of the things you enjoyed and had fun doing before you became a Christian aren't fun anymore. Now that Christ is your Lord, those things seem flat and tasteless to you. Why? Because God is changing you.

Colossians 1:22 uses three words or phrases to describe the change God is making in you. The exact words may vary, depending on the Bible translation you're using, but they have the same meanings. List the three words or phrases you find in your Bible.

1.

2.

3.

No matter what translation you're using, you saw the word *holy*. Maybe you've never considered yourself to be a holy person. Perhaps you don't want to be like some people's false idea of what a holy person is. In the Bible the word *holy* has three meanings that can apply to you and me.

1. *Holy* applies to places where God is present and to people related to those places or to God Himself.
2. The word denotes purity and godliness in God's people.
3. *Holy* describes places, things, and people who've been set apart by God's presence. You're a holy person because God has set you apart from your former, evil ways and has separated you for Himself. He's creating a new purity in you as He helps you clean the old ways—and even the desire for the old ways—out of your life.

By the way, are you using the Scripture-memory card to learn your memory verse for this week? You should have cut this week's card from the back of the book. Put it in a place where you'll see it often. Carry it with you and use it for a quick review when you have a free moment. You should build a packet of memory cards by adding the card(s) for each week to the one you've already cut out.

SURVIVAL KIT

You've already seen that 2 Corinthians 5:17 explains why things are changing in your life. If you were going to use your own experience to explain the meaning of that verse to an unbeliever, what would you say? Take time to think. Then record that explanation here in a short paragraph.

Now read Colossians 1:27. The last part of that verse identifies who's changing your life from old to new. According to Colossians 1:27, where is Christ right now?

Do the two simple words "in you" remind you of what should be written on the palm of the hand drawing you've seen in *Survival Kit?* Write that phrase on the palm of the hand in the drawing.

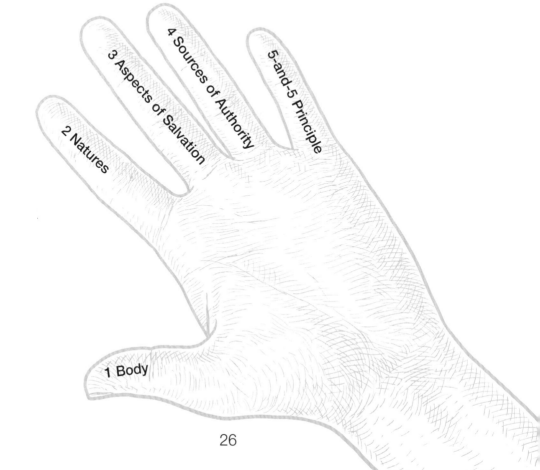

3 Aspects of Salvation

4 Sources of Authority

5-and-5 Principle

2 Natures

1 Body

Christ is "in you." He's "The Indwelling Christ, Controlling All." Because of this truth, your life is changing day by day.

> **What are some habits, thoughts, and feelings that Christ has already changed in your life? They're now flat and tasteless, and you no longer have any desire for them. List them here.**

But you know, some of the old ways really try to hang on, don't they? More than likely, you're still struggling with some habits, thoughts, desires, and feelings that you know shouldn't be a part of your new life in Christ.

> **Meditate on Colossians 1:22 and allow Christ, your Lord, to reveal to you the habits, thoughts, desires, and feelings over which He wants to give you victory today.**

If the victory were easy, you would have gained it long ago. Christ is going to give you His strength to gain the victory. At the same time, you may need a different strategy for applying the strength He's going to give you.

■ Pause now and open your heart to the Holy Spirit.

> **Allow Him to reveal to you what you should do in addition to what you've done in the past or what you should do differently from what you've done in the past. Then complete the following sentences.**

> > I'm trusting Christ to give me strength for the victory over something in my life I'm still struggling with. To use that strength to gain the victory, this is what I'm going to do that I've never done before:

> > This is what I am going to do differently from the way I've done it before:

A Basic Principle to Choose By

Read 1 Corinthians 10:31; Romans 14:7-8.

The Christian faith isn't a long list of do's and don'ts you must observe. And you should beware of people who try to give you such a list. Instead, the Bible gives you a simple principle to follow in making all of life's choices. You'll find that principle stated in 1 Corinthians 10:31.

Read 1 Corinthians 10:31 to discover the principle. Then write the principle in your own words.

The words you used for your answer may not be exactly like someone else's. And that's OK because it's your answer. Whatever you said is correct as long as you expressed the idea that the correct choice is the one that brings the most glory to God.

Now turn back a few pages in your Bible and read Romans 14:7-8.

The apostle Paul wrote these verses, as well as the verse you read from 1 Corinthians. In both cases he was dealing with activities that are doubtful for Christians. And in both cases he made two points very clear.

1. Our conduct is a statement of the life we now have in Christ.
2. All we do should bring glory to God.

Let's look at some choices people in the Bible made and decide whether those choices brought the most glory to God. The Book of Acts says early Christians sold their personal possessions so that they could use the money to meet the needs of other Christians.

Read Acts 4:32–5:2 to learn about a choice that a couple named Ananias and Sapphira made. Then check the box beside the choice you think would have brought the greatest glory to God.
- ☐ Ananias and Sapphira were justified in their choice because it was their possessions they sold in the first place. They were unjustly punished.
- ☐ Ananias and Sapphira should have given everything and shouldn't have misrepresented what they were doing.

☐ Ananias and Sapphira should have asked permission to hold back a portion of the offering to meet their own pressing needs.

John 4:4-42 tells about the Samaritan woman who chose to trust Jesus. Then she ran back to the city and told everyone there about Him.

Read John 4:4-42 and check the box beside the choice you think would have brought the greatest glory to God.

☐ The woman should have recognized her place in the social structure and consulted with the elders in the city before making a decision.

☐ The woman made the choice that brought the most glory to God.

☐ The woman should have respected Jesus' religion and at the same time realized that each person must work out her own faith.

Acts 10:9-16 tells about Peter's vision in which God commanded him to eat animals that his Jewish tradition forbade.

Read Acts 10:9-16. Then check the box beside the choice you think would have brought the greatest glory to God.

☐ Peter was correct in his choice to refuse to eat forbidden meat. For all he knew, God could have been testing his obedience.

☐ Peter should have obeyed God's command without any hesitation.

☐ Peter should have asked God to explain the meaning of the vision so that he would understand what he was supposed to do.

I hope you checked the second choice in each of the examples you studied. Since the moment you became a Christian, you've constantly faced choices about how you'll behave as a Christian. Choosing to respond in a way that most clearly reveals Christ's indwelling presence in your life is always the best response. But knowing which choice is the right one isn't always easy.

■ **Recall a difficult choice you recently had to make.**

Briefly describe that choice.

(Examples: I had to choose whether to accept another responsibility at church. I had to choose whether to engage in a gossip session with friends. I had to choose whether to withhold my offering because of pressing bills.)

Now list at least three choices you could have made. Record the choice you actually made first.

1.

2.

3.

Now circle the choice that would have brought the most glory to God. If you're unable to circle the actual choice you made, take time now to ask for God's forgiveness and ask Him to show you a way you can still glorify Him in that decision.

Remember, God is a loving, understanding Father who loves you in spite of your mistakes. He wants to help you use your mistakes to grow and become a stronger Christian.

What's a choice or a decision you're struggling with right now?

Talk with God about that struggle. Tell Him you truly want to make the choice that will bring the most glory to Him and ask Him to help you know what that choice should be. When you feel that the indwelling Christ has given you the answer, record it here.

You've already learned what a help the Word of God can be in making choices between right and wrong. By now you should have Psalm 119:11 committed to memory. Record it here.

The memory verses printed at the back of *Survival Kit* are quoted from the Christian Standard Bible. If you prefer memorizing from another translation, feel free to do so. You may create your own Scripture-memory cards, using the translation of your choice. Be certain to write the verses word for word.

Review This Week's Study

By this time you should be able to write what should appear on the palm of the hand drawing on this page. Write it if you can. If you need help, review 2 Corinthians 5:17. More important than being able to write the words is actually feeling and knowing that Christ's indwelling presence is more in control of your life now than He was a week ago.

3 Aspects of Salvation

4 Sources of Authority

5-and-5 Principle

2 Natures

1 Body

ONE BODY

ITS LIFE AND SERVICE

How do you feel about your relationships with other believers in the fellowship of your church?

How do you feel about your involvement in the life, ministry, and mission of your church?

How deeply are you committed to other believers, and how strong are the ties of ministry and fellowship among you?

Learning to live in relationship with other Christians in the body of Christ is a key part of being a survivor in your Christian life.

The theme for this week is:

One Body: Its Life and Service

This week you'll learn why your relationship with other Christians in the body of Christ is so important to you. You'll learn why you and your fellow Christians need one another in the fellowship of the body of Christ, and you'll see some of the differences that relationship has already made in your life. You'll also gain a better understanding of some of your responsibilities as a member of the body of Christ.

Being in the Body

Read Romans 12:4-5; 1 Corinthians 12:12-13;
2 Timothy 1:8-10; 1 Peter 2:9-10; Ephesians 4:1-4.

Your personal spiritual growth depends on your being in the body of Christ. There should be no lone-ranger Christians in God's family. Becoming a follower of Jesus Christ is an act of commitment to others who've also vowed to follow Him forever.

Can you imagine a newborn baby being left alone by its family to survive on its own? Hardly! Babies can't survive if left alone. They need constant love, care, and attention. As far as that goes, can you imagine members of a family ever reaching an age when they don't need one another? Hardly! Regardless of age, people need to be surrounded by family—other people who are concerned about their well-being.

The same is true of your spiritual life. You may be a new Christian, or you may have been a Christian for months, even years. Regardless of your spiritual age, you never outgrow your need for the family of God for your survival in the world and for your continued spiritual growth.

> **Romans 12:4-5 states one central truth about the family of God, the church. That truth can be expressed as an equation. Fill in the missing letters, based on what you read in those verses.**

> **M _ _ _ p _ _ _ _ (or members) = one _ _ _ _**

A central truth about the church is its oneness. Verse 5 says, "We who are many are one body in Christ." So you should have written the equation:

Many parts (or members) = one body

When Asian people count on their fingers, they start with the thumb. Can you recall what you've already learned from the hand drawing about the keys to your survival as a Christian?

> **How is the hand labeled across the palm?**
> **How is the thumb labeled? Refer to page 6 if you need help.**

The interplay of meanings is interesting. "The Indwelling Christ, Controlling All" lives in you and in each of your fellow Christians. So all of us together make up the one body of Christ. Christ is in us. And we're in Christ because we're one body in Christ. The thumb on your hand works in cooperation with each finger. In the same way, the truth that we're all the one body in Christ is vital to each of the other truths you'll learn. You must always combine this first truth with the others in order to survive as a growing, fulfilled Christian.

Romans 12:4-5 is your Scripture-memory assignment for this week. It's quoted from the Christian Standard Bible on your Scripture-memory card. Remember, however, that you can memorize it from any translation you wish. In almost any version you use, the four key words will be the same: *many, parts* (or *members), one,* and *body.*

■ **Carefully read 1 Corinthians 12:12-13.**

> **Which of those two verses is more like Romans 12:4-5? In fact, that verse includes the same four key words you saw in Romans 12:4-5. Record the number of that verse here. _____**

> **According to 1 Corinthians 12:13, what was one of the first things the Holy Spirit did for you when you became a Christian?**

In that verse the word *baptized* means "completely submerged." The Holy Spirit doesn't loosely attach you to the edge of Christ's body. He completely immerses you in it. Having natural, healthy growth as a Christian depends on your being deeply involved in the fellowship of a church. The love and nurture you find among other believers provide the climate you need for your spiritual growth.

Understanding what the church is and what the life of the church is like will help you understand why being a part of it is so important. Our word *church* is the translation of the Greek word *ekklesia* (eh-kluh-SEE-ah). In Jesus' day the word referred to a group of citizens who had been called apart for a special meeting or assembly. Now apply that idea to the church. Before you became a Christian, you generally lived the way you wanted to and followed your own desires. Then Christ called you: "Follow Me! Separate yourself from others who live by their personal desires. Be My disciple!" You heard Him and responded, just as I heard and responded and just as every other Christian heard and responded. We came to Christ. We've decided to follow Him. We're called-out ones. We're the church.

> ■ **You'll see the words *called* and *calling* in each of the other three Scripture-reading assignments for today. First review 2 Timothy 1:8-10.**
>
> Who calls us out?
>
> In whom are we called out?
>
> Now turn to 1 Peter 2:9-10. According to those verses, what should called-out ones do?

As called-out ones, we're to proclaim (declare or show forth) the One who has called us out. Perhaps the Good News Translation best expresses how we're to do that. We're to "proclaim the praises of the one who called [us] out of darkness into his marvelous light" (v. 9).

> ■ **List several titles used in 1 Peter 2:9-10 to describe the called-out ones.**
>
> Four titles from verse 9:
>
> One title from verse 10:

The last two descriptions say almost the same thing. Because we're Christians and a part of Christ's church, we're "a people for his possession" (v. 9). We're "God's people" (v. 10), whom He has called "out of darkness into his marvelous light" (v. 9).

■ **Ephesians 4:1-4 describes the character of called-out ones. Christ enables us to live a new lifestyle. List characteristics of this new lifestyle.**

Which of these characteristics would you like to be most visible in your life? Circle that characteristic.

Here's a deep thought: Christ won't give you that characteristic. You see, He *is* that characteristic. Christ is humble, gentle, patient, loving, and all the rest. The way to make that characteristic visible in your life is to let Christ dwell in you and control you. Then persons you meet today will see that lovely part of His nature because He's now living in you and controlling you.

Right now take time to let the Holy Spirit guide you to identify what has been keeping that characteristic from being evident in your life. It may be a thought, desire, habit, or characteristic. Then surrender control of that thought, desire, habit, or characteristic to the indwelling Christ.

Did you notice a familiar two-word phrase in Ephesians 4:4? Notice that verse refers to called-out ones as "one body." Tomorrow you'll continue thinking about this important idea as you learn more about the unity and life of the body of Christ.

Clip out the Scripture-memory card for week 1 and begin memorizing the verses. Use the card for the foundation week to review and reinforce that verse.

DAY 2

Unity and Life in the Body

Read 1 Corinthians 12:4-6,14-27; Acts 2:42-47; 4:32-35; Ephesians 4:11-16.

As you read 1 Corinthians 12:14-27, did you notice anything different from the way Paul usually wrote? If you didn't, read the passage again to catch it.

Jesus often used analogies to teach spiritual truths. He said He's the Vine, and we're the branches (see John 15:5); He's the Shepherd, and we're the sheep (see John 10:11). He called us salt and light and cities set on a hill (see Matthew 5:13-14). However, Paul seldom used analogies in his writings. First Corinthians 12:14-27 is an exception to almost everything else Paul wrote.

In this passage Paul taught a spiritual truth by comparing Christ's called-out ones to the different parts of the human body. He used the way parts of the physical body depend on one another to show that the different parts of Christ's body relate and depend on one another. Though each part is unique, it's connected to the others. The indwelling Christ is equally present in the hand, the foot, or an inner organ. Each one depends on all of the others.

No one part of the body can function or even survive separated from all of the other parts. Just as a hand can't float in the air unattached to an arm, there can't be division in Christ's one body. There's no room for jealousy or conflict between one member of the body and another. (Can you imagine a hand being jealous of an ear or a foot being in conflict with an eye?) What a powerful description Paul gave of life in the body of Christ.

A man once wrote a friend, "Pardon my handwriting; I have a bad case of gout in my foot." Those who've endured the agonizing inflammation of gout can fully understand that pain in the foot can be so intense that even the ability to concentrate enough to write is affected.

Your growth in the Christian life directly depends on those you're related to in the body of Christ. When one suffers, all should share the hurt. When one rejoices, all should be happy.

According to 1 Corinthians 12:18, who decides where each member of the body belongs?

Verse 18 expresses it clearly: "God has arranged each one of the parts in the body just as he wanted."

For most of us, there have been times when we wished we could be like someone else. We wanted to be able to do the things other church members do or hold responsibilities they hold. Be careful! Sometimes these feelings can lead to jealousy, envy, or even conflict. Perhaps you know of times when this kind of jealousy, envy, or conflict has disrupted the harmony among the members of Christ's body. But a member has no reason to be jealous or envious of any other member. God Himself has put each of us where He wants us to be.

■ **Now read 1 Corinthians 12:25-27 one more time, slowly and thoughtfully. Here are two questions for you to consider, based on those verses.**

Is the lifestyle described in these verses unique to called-out ones? Or is it common to find such a spirit also among those who don't believe in Jesus Christ? Explain your answer here.

Missionaries, diplomats, and other people who go to live in foreign countries often experience culture shock when they have to learn and adjust to entirely different ways of thinking, speaking, and doing things. What culture shock did you have to deal with when you became a part of the body of Christ?

Read Acts 2:42-47; 4:32-35.

These passages will boggle your mind if you don't understand the true meaning of the church. These Scriptures don't teach communal living. Nor do they say that all of the Christians sold their belongings and pooled the funds. Rather, the idea expressed in the original language is that from time to time, Christians sold a portion of their assets and shared the proceeds through the apostles to help meet the needs of other Christians.

Those who had more than they needed shared with the needy. As they did, they were confident that God, in turn, would supply all of their needs in the future. Notice also that they shared far more than wealth. They shared their very lives with one another—eating, praying, sharing in Bible study, and teaching. The fellowship you share with other believers is a vital part of your growth in Christ. Don't neglect it! Plunge deeply into the family of God and develop relationships with those who are your new brothers and sisters in the family of faith.

■ **Compare Acts 2:42-47 and Acts 4:32-35.**

Both of these passages describe three important aspects of the church then and now. Read both sets of passages. Then fill in the blanks to complete the summary sentences.

Acts 2	Acts 4	
44	32	*Church members are* _____.
45	34-35	*Church members should* _____.
42-43	33	*Church members should* _____.

■ **Read Acts 2:45 once more.**

Which would be more difficult for you—to sell a personal possession to help a fellow Christian in need or to receive such a gift? Why?

No doubt you recognized that this was another question with no definite, right, or easy answer. Whatever you recorded may indicate ways you need to ask the Lord to help you grow spiritually in relationship with your fellow Christians.

> Acts 2:46 says the early Christians often visited in one another's homes. How could you become a present-day example of that same pattern?

> Checkup time. Notice that the thumb and the palm are blank on the hand drawing. Record the two important truths that are missing. Then turn to page 6 to check your work.

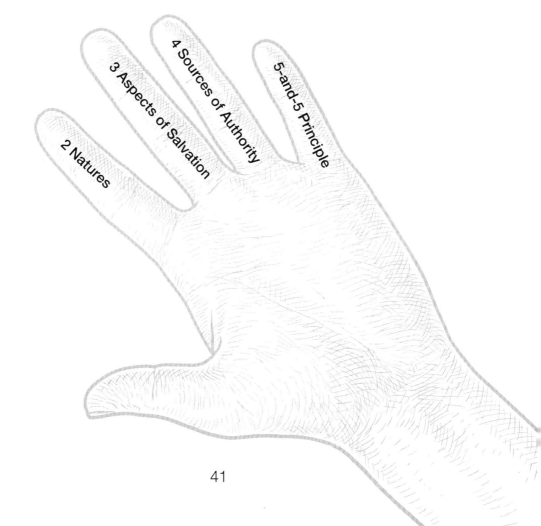

Functioning in Love

Read 1 Corinthians 13:1-13; Ephesians 4:11-16.

First Corinthians 13 is one of the most beautiful chapters in the Bible, as well as one of the most famous passages in world literature. In this chapter you read about the greatest of all realities.

Write that reality below.

The greatest reality:

Love is the greatest reality in the world. God is that love, and Christ lives in you so that you can let it flow to others.

The body of Christ exists to reveal love.

God called you out from being an unbeliever to be changed by the love of Christ. Each day since that time, His love has been changing you to make you more like Him.

Now take a closer look at 1 Corinthians 13. In the first three verses, which of the following qualities are described as being less important than love? Check each box that applies.

- ☐ Great spiritual knowledge
- ☐ Marvelous powers of speaking
- ☐ Being willing to die for truth
- ☐ Generosity to the poor
- ☐ Mighty faith

You should have checked all of the boxes. As great and as important as these qualities are, none are as great or as important as love.

Now find in 1 Corinthians 13:4-7 the many qualities of love that Paul mentioned. List those qualities here.

Circle the quality you think is now most evident in your life. Then underline the quality you would most like to be evident in your life.

Would you be surprised to know that all of these qualities can and should be yours as a Christian? God is love. These qualities of love become more and more apparent in your life as you yield yourself to the indwelling Christ and as His control over your life becomes more complete.

In verses 8 and 13 Paul listed five ideals in addition to love. Place an X beside those that aren't as enduring as love. Place a check mark beside those that aren't as great as love.

☐ Inspired prophecy   ☐ Hope
☐ Faith   ☐ Knowledge
☐ Tongues

Did you use an *X* to indicate that inspired prophecy, tongues, and knowledge will pass away? Did you use a check mark to indicate that faith and hope, as great as they are, aren't as great as love? Love is the greatest thing in the world. That's why God wants His love to flow through you to others.

God did two things when you became a Christian and Christ became your Lord. He added you to His body as a working member. And He began giving you spiritual abilities called gifts. Think of the gifts of the Spirit as riverbeds through which Christ's love flows. The faster a river flows, the deeper the riverbed is cut. As God's love flows through you, your gifts deepen. Their purpose is to let more of Christ's love flow through you to others. He wants you to be a channel of His love to others. That's why He has given you gifts.

SURVIVAL KIT

■ **Read 1 Peter 4:10 and answer the following questions.**

Where did your spiritual gift(s) come from?

What should you do with your spiritual gift(s)?

The most important point to remember about gifts is that they're simply channels to carry Christ's love. Gifts have value only if you let Christ's love flow through them.

You need to understand the difference between spiritual gifts and talents. A spiritual gift is a spiritual ability that God has given to you. The Holy Spirit then empowers you to use that ability for the good of the body and for helping the body function as it should to do God's will. On the other hand, you may have one or more talents—capacities you were born with that you later discovered and developed. Musical ability; computer skills; public speaking; and cooking tasteful, nutritious meals are examples of talents.

The way talents and gifts are used can be both related and different. A spiritual gift can be used only as the Holy Spirit empowers you to use it for the good of the body or for the work of the body. Talents are related to gifts when they become the means by which you express a spiritual gift. Say, for example, you have musical talent. You may use that talent to express a variety of spiritual gifts, such as service, ministry, or teaching. Only Christians have received spiritual gifts, and those gifts can be used only for God's glory. On the other hand, any person can have any number of talents and can use those talents in any way they choose—even for selfish or evil purposes.

List talents you have that you can use to glorify God.

Your Scripture-memory assignment for this week
is Romans 12:4-5. See if you can write it from memory.
Then use your Scripture-memory card to check your recall.

■ **Review 1 Corinthians 12:4-6.**

You should see that each of these short verses shows a contrast or relationship between something that's different and something that's the same. Complete the chart to summarize those three contrasts.

1 Corinthians 12	Different	Same
Verse 4	*Gifts*	*Spirit*
Verse 5		
Verse 6		

You may have used a variety of words, depending on the translation you're using. The Christian Standard Bible expresses it this way:

- Different kinds of spiritual gifts: "There are different gifts, but the same Spirit" (v. 4).
- Different ways of serving: "There are different ministries, but the same Lord" (v. 5).
- Different abilities to perform service: "There are different activities, but the same God produces each gift in each person" (v. 6).

You'll continue studying spiritual gifts tomorrow, but let's review and reinforce what you've learned today. Why does the Lord God, through His Spirit, give you spiritual gifts? Meditate on Ephesians 4:11-16 to discover the answer. I hope you've been using the suggestions I gave you on page 17 for meditating. Take time now to follow those steps.

Is there a truth that should influence what I believe, how I feel, or the way I behave?

Is there an example to follow or avoid?

Is there a command to obey?

Is there a promise to claim?

Let's summarize today's study by reading verse 16 together:

> From him the whole body, fitted and knit together by every supporting ligament, promotes the growth of the body for building up itself in love by the proper working of each individual part.
> **EPHESIANS 4:16**

DAY 4

Gifts in the Body

Read Romans 12:1-8 and 1 Peter 1:13-16.

When you became a Christian, God gave you one or more spiritual gifts to enable you to do the things He wanted you to begin doing immediately as a member of the body of Christ. Some of the gifts God gives are listed in the passage from Romans that you just read. Others are listed in Ephesians 4:11 and 1 Corinthians 12:4-18,28-30. What an impressive list! And we probably shouldn't consider this a complete list by any means.

> **You've already studied most of these verses since you began** *Survival Kit*. **Take time to review Ephesians 4:11 and 1 Corinthians 12:4-18, 28-30 now. As you do, list gifts God may have given you at the time you became a Christian.**

How many of those gifts did you list? Did you notice giving and serving in the lists of gifts you reviewed? I think you could probably add both of these to the list you made if you haven't already listed them. I wouldn't definitely say that you received these two gifts. But I think it would be reasonable for God to give every new Christian the ability to give and serve in some way.

Your most effective use of the gifts God gives you depends on your understanding several important truths about spiritual gifts. Let's look at those truths now.

GOD HAS GIVEN YOU SPIRITUAL GIFTS. We examined this truth in yesterday's study.

GOD ADDS GIFTS AS YOU MATURE SPIRITUALLY. Although you received spiritual gifts at the moment you became a Christian, you didn't receive every gift that God would ever give you. Because some gifts require a higher level of spiritual maturity, they aren't given until you reach that level.

If you're a new Christian, you shouldn't be concerned because you don't have gifts you see in other Christians. You should concentrate on your Christian growth and spiritual maturity. Be patient, trust God's wisdom, and in due time He will give you the additional gifts you need to function in the body as He wishes.

Here's the way it works. If you've been a Christian for several years, you'll probably recognize this as a description of your own experience.

- You continue growing as a Christian and maturing spiritually.
- Your spiritual growth brings you to a level of spiritual maturity where you can assume more responsibility in the body of Christ and perform more difficult tasks.
- God leads you to assume the responsibility or undertake the task, and He gives you the additional gifts as you need them.

If you've been a Christian for several years, you should probably be able to identify additional gifts God has given you as you matured spiritually and were able to assume additional responsibilities in the body.

If you can identify gifts God has given you in addition to the ones He gave you when you became a Christian, list two or more of them here.

A SPIRIT OF OBEDIENCE IS THE KEY TO RECEIVING GIFTS.

Read Romans 12:1-3 again to understand what obedience requires. Here are five key words or phrases from those verses. Look for them as you read.

1. "Transformed"

2. "Conformed"

3. "Sacrifice"

4. "Think of himself more highly"

5. "Will of God"

In the passage you read, two of the five key words or phrases are used to state what you must not do if you're obedient to your Lord. The other three state what you must do.

◼ **Briefly record those five statements, using the five key words or phrases.**

What you must not do:

What you must do:

Now use this example to check what you've written.

What you must not do:

- Be conformed to this world.
- Think of yourself too highly.

What you must do:

- Give yourself as a living sacrifice.
- Be transformed by the indwelling Christ.
- Do the will of God.

First Peter 1:13-16 also speaks of obedience. Read those verses now. In verse 14 what does obedience call you to turn from?

I am called to turn from my _____, which are

caused by my former state of _____.

You may have written "lusts" or "desires" or "passions," depending on what Bible translation you're using. All of these, according to verse 14, were caused by your former state of ignorance.

Now you're no longer ignorant. The indwelling Christ helps you know the will of God. As a member of the one body of Christ, the church, you're learning more and more of what Christ wants you to be and do.

> **The same key word appears four times in 1 Peter 1:15-16. Locate that key word and record it here.**

> **Why would holy living be important to someone who has been entrusted with spiritual gifts?**

Can you imagine how terrible it would be if someone tried to pervert God's gifts by using them in unholy ways?

■ **As a part of your quiet time today, meditate on Romans 12:1-3.**

> **Remember, you can find my suggestions for meditating on Scripture on page 17. As you meditate, focus on areas of your life in which you're struggling to obediently conform to God's will. Can you list reasons you're struggling?**

> **Is God's call to obedience challenging some of your values or priorities? If so, list them here.**

> **Now it's time to check up. Today is the ninth day you've studied your *Survival Kit*. Write the number of days in those two weeks when you've had a quiet time, including prayer and Bible study.**

Tomorrow you'll conclude your study of "One Body" by looking at the body of Christ from a slightly different viewpoint.

DAY 5

The Body Is a Building

Read 1 Peter 2:1-10 and Ephesians 2:19-22.

The Bible uses several figures of speech to describe what the church is. The truth represented by the label on the thumb in the hand drawing is one of the most important of all the figures of speech the Bible uses.

Recall that truth and supply the missing words in the following sentence.

The church is _____ _____ in Christ.

You also learned a Bible verse that speaks of the one body, made up of all people who follow Christ. Fill in the key words that are missing from that verse.

As we have many _____ in _____ _____, and all
the _____ do not have the same function, in the same
way we who are many are _____ _____ in Christ.
ROMANS 12:4-5

Check your Scripture-memory card for that verse to be certain you're correct.

The two passages you read for today's study use a different figure of speech to describe the church.

Can you identify the figure of speech without looking ahead? If not, review the verses and see if you can catch it. Then continue reading.

In these passages the called-out ones are described as a building rather than a body. Christ is "the head of the body, the church" (Colossians 1:18). But He's also "a chosen and honored cornerstone" of the building (1 Peter 2:6). This passage describes each of us as "living stones" (v. 5). We're being constructed into "a spiritual house" (v. 5).

Watching stonemasons build a stone wall is interesting. They chip away at each stone, smoothing and shaping it to make a good fit with the stones around it. There's a spiritual lesson here:

You can't grow as you should
if you aren't part of the church.

God's shaping process in your life requires you to be related properly to other living stones. Don't let this important truth escape you! Just as stonemasons chip away the stones until they fit correctly, God chips away at your character. He molds and shapes until you can be be bonded with other living stones.

Some people have referred to the work the Lord does in your life as the sandpapering process. He gently reshapes you from an isolated stone until you're able to fit snugly with the other stones that make up His spiritual house. Apart from your fellowship with the others who are also "living stones," you'll never become what your Lord wants you to be.

Here are several stones that have rough edges. Read 1 Peter 2:1. According to that verse, what are some of rough edges our Lord may be expected to chip away from our lives as we come to Him? Record them on the stones.

First Peter 2:1-10 mentions two kinds of stones. You and I and all other Christians are like stones with rough edges—envy, hypocrisy, and all of the other evils listed in verse 1. But Jesus Christ, our sinless Savior and Lord, is the chosen, honored, or valuable cornerstone described in verse 6.

Yet this chosen cornerstone may not seem precious or valuable to unbelievers.

According to 1 Peter 2:7-8, what kind of stone does Christ become to those who won't believe in Him?

Thinking of Christ as "a stone to stumble over" (v. 8), as a rock that gives offense to some people, may seem strange to you. But this is the way people see Jesus when they reject Him as their Savior.

Now look again at Ephesians 2:19-22. What's the cement that bonds together the living stones that make up the church?

Isn't it great to know that you and your fellow believers form a building in which God's Holy Spirit lives?

How strongly are you aware that you, as an individual member of the body (or the building) of believers, truly need other called-out ones?

Describe how your relationship with other believers enabled growth in an area of your Christian life.

Now think about an area of your Christian life that needs to develop and grow. Identify it here.

Pray and wait for the Holy Spirit to direct your thinking. Then identify two or more Christians who can support you and help meet your growth needs in those areas. List their names here.

Plan a time to contact each of the people you've listed and express appreciation for the way they're aiding your spiritual growth. Ask for specific prayer, encouragement, and help.

By this point in your study of Survival Kit, *you should have memorized two Scripture passages. Try recording them from memory.*

Psalm 119:11

Romans 12:4-5

Review This Week's Study

Write a brief paragraph explaining the statement that the church is a body.

What's your function in the body?

How are you using your gifts to function effectively as a member of the body?

How are other members' gifts helping you grow as a Christian?

Week 2

TWO NATURES

OLD AND NEW

Do you remember how great you felt about your
new life in Christ when you became a Christian?

And do you remember how quickly Satan used your old nature to try to get back into your life? A slip here. A wrong thought there. Suddenly you realized you were having to struggle with temptations you thought being saved would forever remove from your life.

As long as you live, your old nature will be locked in conflict with your new nature. This week's theme is:

Two Natures: Old and New

You'll learn the secret to winning the victory in your inner conflict with sin. Satan will try to show you how to fake it. He'll try to convince you that it's much easier to simply pretend. But that's no victory. That's surrender to the old nature. The real victory is in surrendering complete control of your will, thoughts, and decisions to the indwelling Christ. That's what you'll learn about this week.

You Belong to Your Choice

Read Romans 8:10-11 and Galatians 2:20; 5:13-18.

Did you know you now have two natures rather than one? From the time you were born, you had an old nature. From the time of your new birth, you've also had a new nature. Your old nature seeks to exalt self; your new nature seeks to let God's love flow through you.

You'll never finish learning everything the Scriptures teach about these two natures. Because you've already lived with the old nature for quite a while, you don't need to learn about it first. Instead, you'll begin this week's study learning about your new nature.

Think of your old nature like the law of gravity. This law is always in effect, pulling you downward. The law of gravity keeps you from flying or floating above the earth for even a few seconds.

Think of your new nature like lift, the force that acts on the wings of an airplane to make it rise from the earth as it moves through the air. That law isn't always in effect. It works only if the conditions are met that cause it to work. In the same way, while your old nature is always working trying to pull you down, your new nature works only when you're doing the things that allow it to work. When the new nature functions in your life, it causes God's love to flow through you and assures you of constant victory over sin. However, the minute you don't allow the new nature to function in your life, the old nature, like the law of gravity, begins pulling you down.

▪ **Review your Scripture-reading assignment for today to see what the Bible says about your two natures.**

Notice that a certain key word appears twice in Galatians 5:13-14. You've already studied this word more than once in your *Survival Kit*. The word tells how your new nature functions in your life.

Record that word here.

Yes, your new nature functions in love. But not your old nature!

According to Galatians 5:15, what are some signs that the old nature is in control? Record them here.

In verse 15 Paul was describing wild animals that bite and hurt one another. Seeing people—especially Christians—act that way is terrible. Paul explained in verse 17 how such a thing can happen:

> The flesh desires what is against the Spirit, and the Spirit
> desires what is against the flesh; these are opposed
> to each other, so that you don't do what you want.
> **GALATIANS 5:17**

Take your pencil and make two changes in the verse I just quoted. Replace the words "the flesh" with "your old nature." Replace the words "the Spirit" with "your new nature." Read the verse aloud as you've changed it.

You decide which nature will be in control of your life. So your choice determines which nature will control your life and which nature will be prevented from controlling your life.

You must meet a certain condition if the law of the new nature is to be in control in your life. That condition is stated in Galatians 5:16. Different translations express that condition with slightly different words:

- "Walk by the Spirit" (CSB, ESV, NIV).
- "Walk in the Spirit" (KJV).
- "Let the Spirit direct your lives" (GNT).

Record in your own words how you would explain the condition that must be met for the new nature to be in control. Later you'll have a chance to change or add to what you've written.

Did you express that the condition is walking by the Spirit or letting the Spirit direct your life?

> *By the way, Galatians 5:16,22-23 is your Scripture-memory assignment for this week. Cut out the card from the back of the book and begin memorizing these verses today.*

Before you became a Christian, the spirit of the old nature directed your life. Your thoughts, motives, impulses, desires, and actions expressed that nature. Walking in the Spirit is being controlled by the Holy Spirit and living out the will of God rather than the desires of the flesh.

Look back at the various translations of Galatians 5:16. What do you notice about the word *Spirit* in each translation?

Yes! When you became a Christian, Christ broke the old nature's rule over your life. He gave you a new nature. The indwelling Christ controls your life through His Holy Spirit. The old nature sought to exalt self; the new nature seeks to cause the love of God to flow through you.

■ **Read Romans 8:10-11.**

Check any of the following statements that describe your condition now that Christ lives in you.

☐ I'm alive.
☐ I can now live a sinless life.
☐ My spirit is experiencing the life of Christ.
☐ I'm now right with God.

You should have checked all of the boxes except the second.

Don't think of your new nature as "it." Galatians 2:20 tells you who (not what) your new nature is. Read the verse to discover who your new nature is. Write that person's name here.

Christ lives within you.

What an awesome statement! And you "live by faith in the Son of God."

What would you say if someone asked you to explain what it means to "live by faith in the Son of God"? Record a short sentence here.

Now contact two Christian friends and compare your statement to the ways they would answer the question.

The indwelling Christ can control your life only when you choose to let Him do so. You must decide to surrender yourself completely to Him. In making that decision, you belong to your choice. You become Christ's and not your own.

Do you remember that the thumb on the hand drawing represents the number 1? The thumb helps you remember the first key to your survival: "One Body"—the fact that you're a part of the body of Christ and the way you relate to it.

The index finger represents the number 2. What truth does that finger help you remember? Record it here.

Jesus Christ is your new nature.

Jesus resides in you, and He has brought the full presence of God's Holy Spirit to live within you. All the power of God is in you because Christ is that power. He has come to cause you to know the victory that God's power makes certain.

Today as you live your life, remember that you belong to your choice. Choose the new nature of Christ as your Lord today. See all He can do to release His love in and through you. Pray now and commit this day to His purposes for you.

DAY 2

Controlled by the Indwelling Christ

Read Colossians 3:1-7; 2 Corinthians 4:6-10; 5:14-18.

Christ lives in you. Christ Himself is the new nature you've received. Often your first impulse it to ask Christ to give your life qualities like love, power, gentleness, and righteousness. He doesn't give you those qualities; He *is* those qualities in you.

The One from whom all these characteristics flow is already living in you. If you surrender your life to His direction, He will cause His life to flow through you. Because His life is the very essence of those qualities, they flow through you as fully as His life does. Moreover, you'll realize that He doesn't simply give you abilities.

Christ gives you Himself—the source of all abilities.

Rather than giving you a glass of water, Christ has given you the well. Instead of giving you the characteristics you want, He has given you the source of those characteristics. That source is Christ Himself—your new nature.

Galatians 5:22-23 lists many characteristics that fill us when we're filled with the presence of the indwelling Christ:

The fruit of the Spirit is love, joy, peace, patience, kindness,
goodness, faithfulness, gentleness, and self-control.
GALATIANS 5:22-23

Circle the qualities you struggle to display in your life.

■ **Colossians 3:1-7 tells more about your new nature. Read those verses now.**

Now read Colossians 2:12-13. What comparison does Colossians 2:12 make to illustrate the meaning of "raised with Christ" in Colossians 3:1?

There are no specific words you should have used, but your answer should reflect the idea that your baptism symbolized the fact that your old life was buried with Christ and that you were resurrected into a new life with Christ. Your baptism didn't give you your new nature. You already had Christ living in you at the time you were baptized. Your baptism was only a picture or symbol of what happened to you when you trusted Christ.

■ **Now compare Colossians 3:3 to the verses you read in yesterday's Scripture-reading assignment.**

Which of those verses is most like Colossians 3:3?

Did you write Galatians 2:20? Do you agree that this verse is closely connected to Colossians 3:3?

In your Scripture-reading assignment for today, Paul calls you to make a personal choice as a Christian—once in Colossians 3:1, again in verse 2, and a third time in verse 5.

How does your Bible state these three choices?

Verse 1:

Verse 2:

Verse 5:

The Christian Standard Bible states those three choices this way:

- "Seek the things above, where Christ is, seated at the right hand of God."
- "Set your minds on things above, not on earthly things."
- "Put to death what belongs to your earthly nature."

No matter how mature you become as a Christian, you'll sometimes want to take control of your new nature and use it to do something you think should be done. But remember, you don't use Christ. Christ uses you! You simply make a choice. You choose to let the nature of the indwelling Christ take control of your spirit, your mind, your emotions, and your body. The commands in Colossians 3:1-7 show your part in the work of the new nature. You simply concentrate on Christ. Then He's free to make His love flow through you, using your gifts to channel His love where He wants it to go.

Two words, *controller* and *container,* have special meanings for you.

Review 2 Corinthians 5:14-18, in which the apostle Paul tells you about these two words and the special meanings they should have for you.

Depending on your Bible version, verse 14 uses the word *control, rule,* or *compel.* According to that verse, the controller of your life should be:

_____ _____ ____ _____

Christ's role as your new nature is to be the controller.

Read 2 Corinthians 4:6-10 to identify a different figure of speech that describes your role in relation to your new nature.

What word in verse 7 describes what's inside this container?

Your role is to be a container, and the indwelling Christ is the treasure inside the container. Because you have the indwelling Christ inside you, you're assured of victory in your life. Verses 8-9 picture that victory as a series of four contrasts.

Which of the victories in verses 8-9 do you need most in your life right now? Or perhaps you have a greater need for another victory. Use your own words to complete the statement:

My greatest need for victory in my life right now is:

You received a new nature when you became a Christian. You're a container for that new nature. And that new nature is Christ.

You're a container for a new life—the life of Christ.

As a Christian, you're no longer to control yourself. Instead, you're to be controlled by the life of Christ. You should give Him freedom to use you. Second Corinthians 4:7 compares you to a clay pot used in Bible times to preserve a valuable document. Of course, you're more than a clay pot. You're a person. God doesn't take away your dignity. Neither do you become a puppet on a string, unable to make choices. Rather, the indwelling Christ, for whom you're the container, brings you to completeness.

Second Corinthians 4:6 is an awesome verse. Jesus Christ's life within you reveals the very nature of God to you. You're a container for Christ, and He's the light that's the very nature of God. Many people have tried to understand God but can't because they aren't willing to become containers for Christ. Only persons who've received the new nature of Christ have the capacity to know God. Don't be alarmed or puzzled when another person feels you're a religious fanatic. Remember that people who are walking in the dark can't possibly see what's evident only in the light.

■ **Based on what you've learned today, what commitment would you like to make today?**

Are there areas of your life you've been trying to control instead of surrendering control to Christ?

Is there a conscious choice you need to make about letting Christ have control of your life today?

Do you need to claim the victory Christ can give you over feelings of being spiritually crushed, forsaken, or destroyed?

Pray about the commitment you'll make today. Then record the commitment here.

DAY 3

Make Christ King

Read Galatians 5:22-25; Romans 6:12-18; 8:26-28.

An apple tree produces apples. It can't produce peaches because by nature it's an apple tree.

Your new nature also produces fruit. That fruit is listed in two verses you should have memorized by now. Record them here.

*Use your Scripture-memory card to check
your memorization of Galatians 5:22-23.*

Notice that the fruit of the Spirit isn't what you do but what you are. In each case the fruit describes character, not activity.

Which of the ninefold fruit of the Spirit is impossible for you to counterfeit in your own strength?

Which of these characteristics seems to be weakest in your life? Circle it in the verses you just recorded.

Do you believe Christ can become all these things in you? Of course He can! Recall when you became a Christian. God promised that if you asked Him to forgive all your sins, He would do it. You asked, and He did it.

Now that He has kept His word, you can be sure He will also do His work in your life. Undoubtedly, you're aware that since you became a Christian, qualities you couldn't counterfeit in your own strength are being revealed in your life. The mere presence of these qualities assures you that Christ is living in you.

Read Romans 8:26-28. According to verse 26, do you have to tell the indwelling Christ that you're spiritually weak in a certain area? Why or why not?

Never let yourself make the excuse "I don't pray much because I don't know how I ought to pray." Christ's indwelling Spirit can express your innermost thoughts in silent prayer if you'll let Him. The Spirit prays for us in "with unspoken groanings."

Romans 8:27 gives you further assurance of the Holy Spirit's help in prayer. Record the same word twice to complete this paraphrase of the verse:

_____, who searches our hearts, understands what the Spirit

means because the Spirit prays only according to the will of _____.

Romans 8:28 states the result when your new nature takes control of your life:

> We know that all things work together for the good of those
> who love God, who are called according to his purpose.
> **ROMANS 8:28**

Mark which of the following statements is more nearly correct.

☐ Everything happens for the good of people who love God.
☐ God works out everything for the good of people who love Him.

Did you mark the second statement? God doesn't cause bad things to happen to you. Neither does He just let things happen. Bad things often happen to you because you or someone else acted outside God's will. Even when those bad things happen, if you'll let God take active control of your life, He will work in that situation for your ultimate good.

SURVIVAL KIT

As a Christian, you must make a simple decision hour by hour, day by day: to crown Jesus Christ as the Lord of your life.

When you make that decision, Christ's nature is in control, producing the fruit of the Spirit in you. You don't have to struggle to be like Jesus. You simply let Him be Himself within you—the indwelling Christ, controlling all.

Sadly, undesirable words and deeds creep into Christians' lives. You're probably aware of instances in your life. How many times have you heard people excuse unchristian behavior and attitudes with "Well, that's just human nature"? This excuse doesn't work for Christians because they aren't supposed to live according to their human nature. Christ is our new nature, and He changes our attitudes and actions day by day.

I'm not saying you don't have a human nature. It's still there, just as it was before you gave your life to Christ.

■ Read what Romans 6:12-18 says about the old nature.

This passage pictures sin as a sort of king who has the power to rule over you. According to verse 12, you choose who will rule over you.

> **Now look at verse 17. According to that verse, what happens to you if you choose sin to be your ruler?**

Who is this King Sin in your life? The easiest way to discover his true identity is to look at the vowel in the middle of the word *sin*. Sin is an *I* problem. When I choose what pleases me, King Sin reigns. I obey sin's lusts, and the members of my body become "weapons for unrighteousness" (v. 13).

You belong to your choice.

If you choose to let Christ reign, He who's your new nature will cause His fruit to flow from your life. If you choose to give your body to King Sin (who in reality is King I), you become a servant or slave of that king. Under the control of King I, all you can expect is the result of disobeying God.

Your old nature is your human nature. It's the nature of sin within you. It wasn't destroyed when you became a Christian. Rather, for the first time it was dethroned. For the first time sin had no power to control you … except when you chose to become a slave to it again.

■ Check to see whether you understand.

Who's the new nature within you?

Who's the old nature within you?

Who decides which nature will reign over you?

The Christian Standard Bible translates Romans 6:12-13 this way:

> Do not let sin reign in your mortal body, so that you obey its desires.
> And do not offer any parts of it to sin as weapons for unrighteousness.
> But as those who are alive from the dead, offer yourselves to God, and
> all the parts of yourselves to God as weapons for righteousness.
> **ROMANS 6:12-13**

You must not let "any parts" of yourself (v. 13) be ruled by King Sin. You must let "all the parts of yourselves" (v. 13) be ruled by the indwelling Christ.

Do you see how Romans 6:12-13 illustrates the statement "You belong to your choice"? Remember that King Sin is dethroned but not dead.

What do you think Romans 6:18 means by the statement that you've become a servant or a slave of righteousness?

A key word appears several times in verses 16-17. What's that word?

Obey, obeyed, obedient, obedience—whichever form of the word you wrote, its meaning is clear: Either you choose to obey the sinful self, your old nature, or you choose to obey Christ, your new nature.

You become a slave to whichever nature you obey.

Are there areas of your life in which you need to make the conscious choice to dethrone self and enthrone Christ? Take time now to meditate and pray. Allow the Holy Spirit to reveal the areas of your life in which you need to make Christ the King. Then bow before Him and ask Him to be the indwelling Christ in those areas, beginning right now. Tell Him you'll live in a way that shows He's the King in those areas also.

No Reformation

Read Romans 7:15,18-25; 8:5-9; Galatians 5:19-21,24-25.

Romans 7:15,18-21 pictures a Christian who attempts to reform the old nature. Summarize the struggle in your own words.

Did you write something like this?

- "I want to do good, but I can't do it."
- "I don't want to do evil, but I do it anyway."

In what ways can you identify with the struggle you've just summarized? Take time to think before you record your answer.

It doesn't seem logical that Christ would give you His indwelling life, yet you live in such a struggle. However, the struggle is a reality because your old nature can't be reformed. When a tree has apple roots, the branches produce apple fruit. The nature of the root always determines the nature of the fruit. Your old nature still attempts to produce the same kind of fruit it produced before you became a Christian.

Galatians 5:22-23 lists the fruit of the new nature. List that fruit here.

Now read Galatians 5:19-21 and list the fruit of the old nature.

Count the number of deeds related to the old nature that you personally experienced before you became a Christian. Record that number here.

Now count the number of deeds related to the old nature that you've experienced since you became a Christian. Record the number here.

What observation can you make after comparing the two numbers?

Many Christians tend to trust their old nature too far. They assume that giving their lives to Christ automatically removed everything that might lead them astray. Big mistake! They forget that the old nature can't be changed and can't be trusted.

It's a little like two former alcoholics. Both had kicked the habit, as far as they or anyone else could tell. But one of them was so proud of himself that he took just a little drink to show that he knew when to stop. As a result, he returned to alcoholism. The other knew better than to trust himself. He avoided times, places, and situations when the temptation to start drinking again might be too great.

In your opinion, why do people so easily trust the old nature after becoming Christians?

Perhaps you wrote that we don't take sin seriously enough or that sin uses our tendency to trust the old nature as a way of regaining control of our lives. Sometimes Christians have to take some pretty hard blows before they realize they can't ever place confidence in their old nature again. *Self, I, sin*—all of these are words for the old nature.

The old nature will never be any different but will always produce the same ugly fruit.

Because the old nature isn't dead, a civil war rages within you daily. Your new nature and your old nature constantly struggle with each other.

■ Read Romans 7:22-25.

These verses describe the struggle of a Christian who hasn't made a clear-cut decision to let the indwelling Christ be the Lord of his life.

Romans 7:23 mentions a frequent result of war: captivity. And Romans 7:24 pictures a hideous situation. Ancient conquerors developed a terrible way of torturing prisoners. They bound a corpse to a prisoner so tightly that the living man, if he tried to escape, would have to carry the dead man on his back.

> In verse 24 the apostle Paul asked a question that shows he may have been thinking about this horrible torture. What's the question?

> "Who will rescue me from this body of death?" Paul pleaded. Verse 25 gives both the name and the title of the One who can release you from this internal civil war. Record them both here.

> Name: _____ _____

> Title: _____

What significance does this title have in bringing an end to the civil war between your two natures?

If Jesus Christ is truly your Lord, He must control your life. You must submit to His lordship and refuse to obey your old human nature.

■ **Another expression for "the old nature" is "the flesh." Remember what these terms mean and read Romans 8:5-6.**

These two verses contrast two types of life you can experience as a Christian. One is the life of a Christian who has yielded to the rule of the old nature. The other is the life of a Christian who has yielded to the rule of the new nature.

Complete the chart to show the contrast.

	The Old Nature	The New Nature
Mindset (v. 5)		
Results (v. 6)		

■ **Romans 8:7-8 makes four negative statements about a Christian who hasn't yet fully yielded his or her life to the indwelling Christ. Complete these four phrases about that kind of person.**

• Is _____ toward God.

• Doesn't _____.

• Can't _____.

• Can't _____ _____.

Your four phrases should be something like this.

- Hostile (or an enemy) toward God.
- Doesn't subject himself to God's law. Actions are disobedient to God's law.
- Can't subject herself to God's law. Incapable of obeying God's law.
- Can't please God.

What conclusions have you reached about your life as you studied Romans 8:5-8?

Romans 8:9 tells you that the Spirit of God dwells in you. The word *dwell* means "to reside permanently."

Is there any time or area in your life in which Christ doesn't reign as Lord? Explain your answer.

You may have had difficulty putting your answers to the two previous questions into words. Remember that even when you can't put your feelings into words, you can pray about them. Christ's indwelling Spirit will understand your feelings and express them to God for you.

To conclude your quiet time today, meditate on those two questions and pray.

DAY 5

Victory through Surrender

Read Ephesians 4:22-24; Matthew 5:21-22,27-28;
Philippians 4:7-8; Romans 8:37-39; 6:1-11.

In Ephesians 4:22 Paul referred to a deliberate decision Christians make to lay aside or put off the old nature. The picture is of a person who has been wearing a suit of clothes for a long time. Then, in an intentional act, the person takes off the old clothes and lays them aside, not to be worn again.

That kind of decision settles the outcome of the civil war going on within you. The old nature is still alive and active in you. However, its power is rendered helpless when you decide to lay it aside. Choosing to make a permanent commitment to Jesus Christ allows His full power to be active in you.

In Ephesians 4:23 Paul spoke of your mind being renewed. Jesus also made an interesting connection between our thoughts and our actions. Read what He said in Matthew 5:21-22,27-28. According to Jesus, where does every action begin?

Did you say something like "in your mind" or "with a thought"?

In your opinion, what can you do to renew your mind? Paul gave good advice in Philippians 4:7-8. Summarize those verses here.

The Christian Standard Bible expresses Paul's advice this way:

> The peace of God, which surpasses all understanding, will guard your hearts and minds in Christ Jesus. Finally brothers and sisters, whatever is true, whatever is honorable, whatever is just, whatever is pure, whatever is lovely, whatever is commendable—if there is any moral excellence and if there is anything praiseworthy—dwell on these things.
> **PHILIPPIANS 4:7-8**

Did your summary of the verses include all of these ideas?

■ Read Romans 8:37 to find out what Christ will give you when you make Him the Lord and Master of your life.

What kind of victory do you experience, or what kind of conqueror do you become?

Romans 8:38-39 continues the same thought with the assurance that nothing in the world can separate you from the love of God through Jesus Christ your Lord. Note especially that verse 38 says nothing in life can separate you from Christ. You may sometimes feel that life situations are your greatest hindrances as you try to live in your new nature. Christ is victorious over all situations you face. You need only to invite Him into those life situations, whatever they may be, and let His mighty power work. That's what prayer is for.

The apostle Paul made clear that a Christian has no excuse to live with the old nature still in control.

■ Read Romans 6:1-2.

What unanswerable question did Paul ask in verse 2?

In Romans 6:3-5 Paul explained that baptism is a public confession of something that has already taken place in your life. What's that confession?

In baptism you confess that your old, sinful self is dead and that you've been raised to new life in Christ. According to Romans 6:6-7, what happened to free you from the power of the old nature?

Paul said your old nature was crucified with Christ. How, then, did Paul describe your life as a Christian in Romans 6:8-11?

Paul gave the key to living with the new nature in control.

■ **Read Romans 6:12-13.**

Explain the key in your own words.

You can't fake the life of Christ, who's your new nature, by trying to make your old nature behave differently.

Rather, you must constantly choose against your old nature. Trying to be like Jesus is an impossibility. Instead, you must let Jesus Christ become the reigning King of your life. You must give Him the right to guide your thoughts and to control your actions. When you do that, you settle once and for all the fact that He came into your life to be your Lord, the One to whom you belong.

Being a Christian isn't just doing something. It's primarily containing Someone. Christ is in you. He's your new nature. When you deliberately choose to let Him be the leader of your life—your words, your habits, your thoughts, your everything—He becomes the resident King of your existence. The spiritual gifts He gives you will flow through your life. You'll know that the life you're living isn't your life but His.

Imagine that you want to be a great football player. Although you don't have what it takes, you still try with all your might. But your best isn't enough. You've given it your best shot, but you know you've failed.

Then on the sidelines a man walks up to you and introduces himself. Your heart leaps into your throat! He's one of the greatest football players of all time. He offers to do a strange thing. He explains that he has the power to take his strength out of his body and place it in yours. He also offers to put his knowledge of the game into your mind and to give you all the skill he has developed.

You agree to the offer! In a moment you're back on the field, passing with more accuracy and running with more speed than you ever dreamed you could. Your mind races through the plays; you recall every one. The crowd cheers you! You're playing the game of a legendary hero.

Yet in your heart you know why you're playing such a brilliant game. You have the power, skill, knowledge, and strength of the most famous football player of all time implanted in your life. You're humbled by the experience. Others may applaud you, but you know the true source of your performance.

Christ will do exactly that for you, for the rest of your life. You belong to your choice. Crown Him Lord of your life—today, tomorrow, and forever.

Christ guarantees you overwhelming victory!

What situations are defeating you on life's playing field? Imagine that a time-out has been called. Your coach calls you to the sidelines and asks, "What's going wrong out there?" Record your answer here.

Then the coach says, "Can't you see that those things wouldn't be happening if you were following my game plan instead of calling the plays the way you want to? Listen to me, and I'll tell you again what you need to do differently to stop the opponent from defeating you."

Think about the areas of defeat you listed. Take time to pray and meditate. Let Jesus Christ, your Coach, tell you what you need to do to follow His game plan today to gain the victory. Record the game plan you'll follow today.

Now pray and surrender the life you'll live today to the Coach who wants to play His game plan through you.

Review This Week's Study

This week you examined the continuing conflict between the old nature and the new nature in your life. You also learned the secret to ensure that the new nature will be victorious over the old nature.

What's the old nature?

Who's the new nature?

Briefly describe the purpose the old nature is trying to accomplish in your life.

Briefly describe the purpose the new nature is trying to accomplish in your life.

What does the phrase "You belong to your choice" have to do with your inner conflict with sin?

How has the fruit of the new nature in your life changed the way you make choices and the way you relate to others?

THREE ASPECTS OF SALVATION

BEGINNING, PROCESS, AND COMPLETION

Last week you learned that the old nature is still with you, and you saw that Satan uses that old nature to try to paralyze your spiritual life. Satan uses that continuing conflict to hit you broadside with doubts about your relationship with Christ. You even may have wondered, *Am I really saved?*

Another key challenge you must overcome as a growing Christian is the doubt you may have about your salvation experience.

The theme for this week is:

Three Aspects of Salvation:
Beginning, Process, and Completion

You'll see that becoming a Christian is only the beginning point in a process that will continue throughout your life. Your final triumph over sin will come at last when Christ returns and gives you your inheritance.

Three Parts of One Event

Read Philippians 1:3-11.

Perhaps when you took Christ as your Lord and Savior, you thought your simple prayer of surrender would give you all Christ had to offer. Well, you were right!

In that moment you became a forgiven, freed, Christ-indwelled child of God. That happened in the past. In that same moment, however, you also received from God certain rights, and you were given an inheritance. Those rights are yours to claim in the present. You'll receive the inheritance in the future.

Salvation, therefore, comes to you in three stages: past, present, and future. The apostle Paul knew this truth and explained it to his Christian friends in Philippi. You just read what he wrote to them in Philippians 1:3-11.

What did Paul do every time he remembered his Christian friends in Philippi (see verse 3)?

When Paul thanked God for the Philippian Christians, what emotion did he always feel when he prayed (see verse 4)?

As Paul prayed with joy, what was it about these Christian friends that he thanked God for (see verse 5)?

Because the Philippians had been Paul's partners (helpers or fellow workers) in spreading the gospel, where did he say he held them (see verse 7)?

Paul's feelings of love and affection in his heart were so strong that he compared his emotions to whose love and affection (see verse 8)?

Because Paul felt an affection for the Philippian Christians like the love of Christ Jesus, he wanted to be sure they understood the three aspects of salvation. No other verse in the Scriptures summarizes them more completely than Philippians 1:6.

Philippians 1:6 is your Scripture-memory assignment for this week. Clip the Scripture-memory card from the back of the book and begin memorizing.

The chart on this page shows another way of looking at what Philippians 1:6 means. The middle column stands for a process of time. Each of the side columns stands for an event. The words in the chart are quoted from the Christian Standard Bible.

Use your own translation to fill in the second line of each column, recording words from Philippians 1:6 that match the three aspects of salvation—past, present, and future.

The Beginning Point	A Process of Time	The Final Event
"He who started a good work in you …"	*"will carry it on to completion …"*	*"until the day of Christ Jesus."*
" _____ "	" _____ "	" _____ "
Freed from the penalty of sin	*Freed from the power of sin*	*Freed from the presence of sin*
Cleansed by Christ's blood	*Liberated by Christ's indwelling life*	*Given your inheritance by Christ's second coming*

Ann remarked to Tom, who had been a Christian for many years, "Conversion is the end of salvation." Tom didn't understand that Ann was using the word *end* to mean the aim, result, or object of salvation. Strongly disagreeing, he snorted, "The end? Then it must be the front end!"

The chart you completed shows what Tom meant. When you received Christ as your Savior, you were at the beginning end of your salvation. There was much more to come, and there still is!

You know you're a child of God. But you don't know all Christ still has in store for you.

You already possess your salvation, but knowing what you possess allows you to enjoy it.

Let's review what you've learned in *Survival Kit* by completing the hand drawing on this page. See if you can supply all the missing information. See page 6 if you need help.

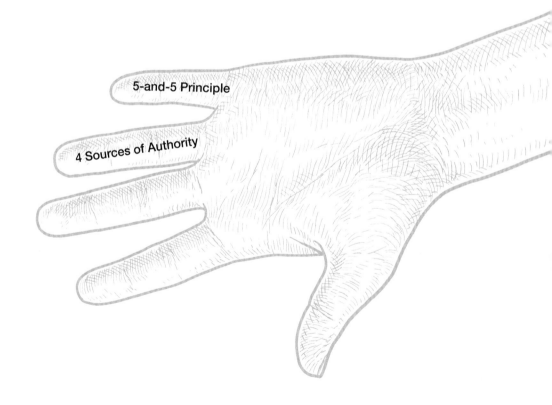

5-and-5 Principle

4 Sources of Authority

The central truth or principle that makes all the others work should be written on the palm. "The Indwelling Christ, Controlling All" placed you in a new relationship when you became a Christian. You should have written this principle on the palm.

The thumb should remind you that you're a part of "One Body in Christ." However, being in the body doesn't mean your life as a Christian will be free of struggles with temptation. So last week you studied the principle of "Two Natures." You should have written that principle on the index finger. Now write the theme for this week on the middle finger.

What has your salvation provided for your daily life since you became a Christian? Even if you've been a Christian for only a few days, you should be able to compose a list. The longer you've been a Christian, the longer your list should be. List some of the results that come to your mind.

Now use the steps you learned on page 17 to meditate on Philippians 1:9-11. Identify at least one teaching or example you should follow. Promise God you'll follow it in your life today.

DAY 2

The Beginning Event

Read Ephesians 1:12-13; 2:3-6,8-10,12-13,17-19.

All of the Scripture verses in today's study relate to salvation past—the moment when you asked Christ to enter your life as Lord and Savior.

> **According to the verses you just read from Ephesians 2, what did God do at that moment? Verse 5 states the answer in two ways. Record both of them here.**
>
> 1.
>
> 2.

Did your answer reflect the ideas that God made you alive together with Christ and that He saved you by His grace?

> **Verse 6 provides two more descriptions of what God did in the moment of your salvation. Record them here.**
>
> 1.
>
> 2.

God "raised us up with him and seated us with him in the heavens in Christ Jesus."

> **What's the significance of the words *we* and *us* in verses 5-6? Ephesians 2:19 should give you a clue.**

> **Do you remember what you studied in week 1? What should you remember when you look at the thumb in the hand drawing?**

According to Ephesians 2:8-9, what did you do to deserve God's forgiveness through Christ?

I hope you understood Ephesians 2:8-9 clearly enough that you wrote, "Nothing."

Now read Ephesians 2:12-13. What does the Bible mean when it says, "You who were far away have been brought near by the blood of Christ" (verse 13)?

Ephesians 2:17-18 makes the matter clear. To whom were you given instant, constant access at the moment you trusted Christ?

You have access to God the Father through Christ.

Now review Ephesians 2:3,5,12,17. What was your condition up until the time Christ set you free from the penalty of sin? See how many characteristics of your life you can list.

Ephesians 2 lists some of the characteristics you may have written. Beside each one, record the number of the verse in which it's mentioned.

Fleshly desires: verse ___   Dead: verse ___

Far away: verse ___   Without hope: verse ___

Without God: verse ___   Without Christ: verse ___

If you need to check your answers, they're printed at the end of today's study.

You'll never stop being amazed at what Christ did for you in that single moment when you prayed and asked Him to enter your life. He called you out of a world in which self ruled over all your decisions. He instantly forgave all the sin and wrong deeds you had ever done. He placed His own life inside yours and began to claim your existence as another part of His kingdom. In a moment of time, you were forever set free from the worry that at the end of life, you'd be separated from God. Those matters are forever settled.

Nothing can take away the new life you received in Christ. You're His forever!

In Ephesians 1:11-13 Paul drew an interesting figure of speech from the age in which he lived. In Bible times a property holder often used a seal or stamp engraved with his personal sign to indicate his ownership. As a mark of his ownership, he pressed the seal or stamp into something soft, such as clay or wax, and attached it to his property. Sometimes the stamp or seal was set into a signet ring the owner wore.

Here's the way the Christian Standard Bible relates the figure of speech:

> In him we have also received an inheritance, because we were predestined according to the plan of the one who works out everything in agreement with the purpose of his will, so that we who had already put our hope in Christ might bring praise to his glory. In him you also were sealed with the promised Holy Spirit when you heard the word of truth, the gospel of your salvation, and when you believed.
> **EPHESIANS 1:11-13**

How were you sealed in Christ?

The Holy Spirit is God's seal on you, proving that you belong to Him.

We're going to complete a chart similar to the one we completed yesterday. Use Ephesians 2:8-10 to fill in the blanks in the chart on the following page.

How You're Saved	*"You are saved by _____ through _____."* *"It is God's _____."* *"For we are his _____."*
Why	*"Created in Christ Jesus for _____ _____"*
How You Aren't Saved	*"This is not from _____."* *"Not from _____."*
Why Not	*"So that no one can _____."*

Did you notice that Ephesians 2:8-10 relates to two of the three aspects of salvation? The section "How You're Saved" speaks of salvation past—the moment when, by grace through faith, you received the gift of God and became a new product of God's workmanship. The section "Why" speaks of salvation present; the indwelling Christ, controlling all, now enables you to do the good works for which you were created.

I'm going to ask you to meditate on a passage of Scripture to conclude your quiet time. By this time you should be familiar with four questions to use in meditating. Try to list them from memory.

1.

2.

3.

4.

If you need to check your answers, see page 17. However, if you need to check your answers, I'm afraid meditating on Scripture isn't yet a regular part of your daily quiet time. I want to encourage you to be more determined to include this essential element in your daily quiet time. Meditating on Scripture is a primary way God is able to speak to you through His Word.

Conclude your quiet time by meditating on Ephesians 2:8-10. Pray that God will reveal His will for your life today. Then commit to follow His leadership.

Answers to exercise on page 91:
fleshly desires (verse 3), dead (verse 5), far away (verse 17), without hope (verse 12), without God (verse 12), without Christ (verse 12)

The Continuing Process, Part 1

Read Romans 5:6-11; 6:17-18; Hebrews 2:14-15,18; 4:14-16.

The warden told a prisoner, "Good news! The governor has given you a full pardon." The delighted prisoner asked when he would be released from his cell. "Oh no!" replied the warden. "We can't release a man like you. You must stay in your cell until you finish your sentence."

At the moment you asked Christ to forgive you and trusted Him to save you, He pardoned you; He delivered you from the condemnation and penalty of sin. That's salvation past, which you studied yesterday. At the same time He forgave you and saved you, He made available to you His power to set you free from the influence and control sin has over your life.

> Not only has Jesus pardoned you, but He has also opened the cell where the old nature held you captive and controlled your thoughts and actions. That's salvation present.

Let's examine Romans 5:6-11 to see how the passage depicts the three aspects of salvation—especially salvation present.

■ **Look at Romans 5:6-8.**

Which aspect of salvation do these verses describe?

Past   Present   Future

Which aspect did Paul switch to at the end of verse 9?

Past   Present   Future

Verses 6-8 speak of salvation past. In the middle of verse 9, Paul switched to salvation future. He ended verse 10 with a clear reference to salvation present.

> **Christ's death is the basis of salvation past. What's the basis of salvation present? Use Romans 5:10 to complete the following sentence.**
>
> **By Christ's death I've received salvation past. Now, through**
>
> **Christ's _____, I daily receive salvation _____.**

Through Christ's life you daily receive salvation present.

> **Reading Romans 5:10 should remind you of Galatians 2:20, which you studied in day 1 last week in connection with your new nature. Take time to review what you learned. What similar thoughts do you see in these two verses?**

You should have expressed the idea that Romans 5:10 says you're saved by Christ's life. Galatians 2:20 says Christ lives in you, and you now live by faith in Him.

Let's review three important truths you've already learned and see how they relate to salvation present—your continuing process of salvation.

1. Satan will stop at nothing to defeat your efforts to grow and serve your new Master.
2. When you became a Christian, your old nature didn't cease to exist. Rather, Satan continues to use your old nature to struggle against your new nature. That struggle is his attempt to introduce crippling sins into your life and defeat you.
3. The key to victory over sin is your surrender to the indwelling Christ. As He controls your life, He gives you daily victory over Satan's attempts to use your old nature to defeat you. This daily victory is salvation present.

■ **Read again a passage you studied last week, Romans 6:12-18.**

Check all of the following statements that the passage supports.

- ☐ Christians should seek to live lives that are consistent with the example and teachings of Christ.
- ☐ Christ has broken sin's power to dominate and control your life.
- ☐ The choice of who will control your thoughts and actions is up to you.
- ☐ Failure to let Christ control your life means you aren't a Christian.

You should have checked all of the statements except the last. The emphasis in Romans 6 is that when we become Christ's servants (slaves), He takes over. Our new Master wants us to live our lives in true holiness. Each day we allow Him to control us, He delivers us from the power and domination of the old nature.

Hebrews 4:14-16 pictures Jesus in a way the Jewish people could easily understand. The Jewish high priest went into the sanctuary and offered sacrifices for the forgiveness of their sins.

■ **Reread Hebrews 4:14-16.**

What kind of high priest does this passage say Jesus is, and where has He gone?

Jesus is our great High Priest who has gone into the heavens, that is, "into the very presence of God" (Hebrews 4:14, GNT).

According to verse 15, how does this great High Priest feel about the temptations you encounter, and why does He feel that way about them?

Jesus sympathizes with you. He's touched by your weaknesses because He Himself was tempted in every way you are. But notice the crucial difference between Jesus and everyone else who has ever lived. He didn't sin when He was tempted.

According to Hebrews 4:16, what are you able to do because of Jesus' sympathy and understanding?

You can go to God confidently and without fear to ask for the strength you need to resist temptation.

■ **Now read Hebrews 2:14-15. According to the first part of verse 14, what did Jesus do so that He could understand you perfectly?**

Jesus took part in your human nature; He shared the same flesh and blood you do.

To what length did Jesus go in order to personally experience everything you, as a human being, must endure? One stark, five-letter word in the middle of verse 14 gives the answer.

In addition to becoming flesh and blood and enduring all you might have to endure in life, Jesus actually shared the human experience of death! Therefore, there's nothing in your life that He hasn't faced personally.

■ **Read Hebrews 2:18.**

Neither the power of death nor the fear of death can hold sway over you, because Christ lives in you. Someone has said, "It's impossible to lead another person to climb a mountain that you yourself have never climbed." Verse 18 makes a clear, precise statement about where Jesus has been in the vast range of human experiences.

> According to that verse, how can you be certain Jesus will fully understand your temptations and suffering?

> Because Jesus has suffered and been tempted, He's able to help you when you're tempted. Record one problem or temptation you're facing today.

> Take at least five minutes to meditate on 1 Corinthians 10:13 in light of what you've just written. Do you believe Jesus understands that situation and can help you with it?

> Yes   No

> Pray with confidence, asking God to help you with that situation today.

The Continuing Process, Part 2

Read Ephesians 5:18; John 7:37-39; Philippians 2:12-13; Hebrews 13:20-21.

The indwelling Christ brings victory to every part of your life. He was tested in every way you might be, yet He didn't sin. He won't permit you to be tempted beyond your capacity. He will always give you a way to escape. Jesus not only protects you but also provides all of the resources you need to be victorious over trials and temptations in daily life.

Ephesians 5:18 is a startling verse! The verb translated "be filled" actually means "be intoxicated"! One result of drinking too much wine is an obvious change in behavior. In this verse Paul was saying, "Be so full of the Holy Spirit that there's an obvious difference in your behavior." Just as drinking alcohol changes who you are and what you are, being filled with the Holy Spirit brings about radical, obvious changes in the way you think and behave.

Let me point out two important things about the Greek word used in the original text of Ephesians 5:18, which is translated "be filled."

- The verb is an imperative—an order, a command.
- It's a verb form expressing continual action: "continue being filled" or "keep on being filled."

So, you see, being filled isn't optional for a Christian.

> You're ordered to continually be so filled
> with the Holy Spirit that the difference
> in your thoughts and actions is obvious.

John 7:37-39 records something very similar that Jesus said. According to these verses, who gives you this "drink" (verse 37)?

What drink was Jesus speaking of?

What's the result of drinking the Holy Spirit?

"Streams of living water" (verse 38) flowing from your life—what a beautiful picture! Do you remember what you learned about the spiritual gifts God gives you? They're channels or riverbeds for Christ's love to flow through you to others.

> **Stop and think about the connection between John 7:37-39 and your ability to be a riverbed through which God's blessings flow to others.**

> **What Jesus said in John 7:38 should also remind you of one of the two points I made about the verb translated "be filled" in Ephesians 5:18. Can you figure out what the relationship is?**

Streams of living water flow continually, don't they? And Ephesians commands you to continually be filled with the Spirit of Christ. Salvation present is guaranteed by Christ. He offers you an unending supply of His Spirit. Whenever you're thirsty, you need only come to Him and drink. The result will be Christ's Spirit filling your personality with His life. Streams of living water will flow from your life and bless the lives of others.

■ Read Philippians 2:12-13.

Does a command to "work out your own salvation" (verse 12) seem inconsistent with all we've said about letting Christ have control and permitting Him to live through you to do all the things you can't possibly do? Not at all!

Notice the two ways the word *work* is used in these verses. God is working in you to enable you to do what fully pleases Him (see verse 13). However, you must work out what God is working into you. You must choose to let the indwelling Christ control you. You must be committed to being an open channel through which His love flows to others.

Look again at Philippians 2:12. Why are you to work out your salvation present "with fear and trembling"? Certainly not because you fear being punished by an angry God. No, it must mean something else.

Check all of the statements you think could help explain the phrase "with fear and trembling."

- ☐ You should live with a humble frame of mind.
- ☐ You always should be aware of your weaknesses.
- ☐ You must constantly try to trust Christ more and serve Him better.
- ☐ The fear of being unfaithful to God is a healthy fear we all should have.
- ☐ You should always have a sense of awe at the way God provides for your needs.
- ☐ You should be genuinely fearful of not allowing Christ to control you in such a way that you fail to receive from Him what He alone can provide.

You should have checked all of the statements as explanations of what it means to work out your salvation present "with fear and trembling."

■ **Now read Hebrews 13:20-21.**

What will God equip you to do or make you perfectly able to do?

Through whom does God enable you to do His will?

Recognize the fact that salvation present is yours today. Your victory rests on the fact that Christ lives in you, and He has experienced every stress and need you now experience. And God is working in your life right now through the power of this same Jesus Christ who's living in you.

Identify an occasion when you were so completely controlled by the Holy Spirit that the effect on your behavior and/or speech was obvious.

Meditate on Philippians 2:12-13. Then record the message God had for you today in that passage.

■ **Now let's review.**

Your Scripture-memory assignment for this week is Philippians 1:6. See if you can record the verse from memory.

Can you remember the key phrase that identifies the key truth you're studying this week? Use it to label the middle finger of the hand drawing. Then try to label the other fingers. Use page 6 to check your work.

4 Sources of Authority

5-and-5 Principle

The Indwelling Christ, Controlling All

The Final Event

Read Ephesians 1:13-14; 1 Peter 1:3-9; 1 Thessalonians 4:15-18.

Will you ever be rid of the old sin nature? Will the time ever come when your new nature doesn't have a daily struggle with the old nature? Yes! When Christ comes again, you'll be set free from the presence and influence of the old nature.

Read 1 Corinthians 15:50-57, one of the most striking passages the apostle Paul ever wrote. Then on the chart draw lines connecting the statements to the verses that support them.

THREE TENSES OF SALVATION	
Your future salvation will come at a point in time.	*Verses 51-52*
Death is connected with sin.	*Verses 55-56*
You can't inherit the kingdom of God with the old nature still in you.	*Verse 50*
You're guaranteed immortality when the old nature has been removed.	*Verses 53-54*
This is all the work of Jesus Christ, not the result of your good deeds.	*Verse 57*

Earlier this week you learned from Ephesians 1:13 that you received the Holy Spirit at the moment you gave your life to Christ. Read that verse again and continue reading through verse 14.

Do you see the important truth verse 14 adds? The Holy Spirit, whom you received at the moment of salvation past, is also a down payment on much more that God has reserved as your inheritance. When you purchase a house, you make a down payment, a cash pledge of the full amount due, to be paid at a future time when you take the house into your personal possession.

What a striking illustration of salvation future! The down payment of your inheritance has already been paid. You have the Holy Spirit.

One day Christ will take you to Himself. He will redeem His purchased possession. And when He does, you will receive the totality of your salvation.

■ **Carefully read 1 Peter 1:3-5.**

Do these verses speak of your salvation past or your salvation future?

☐ Salvation past   ☐ Salvation future
☐ Salvation past and future   ☐ Neither past nor future

The correct answer, of course, is that these verses refer both to what Christ has already done for you (salvation past) and to what He will do in the future.

■ **Look at 1 Peter 1:6-9.**

Which of the three aspects of salvation do you see in these verses?

☐ Salvation past   ☐ Salvation future
☐ Salvation present   ☐ All of these

Do you agree that "All of these" is the best answer? These verses refer to your faith in Jesus Christ, whom you've never seen with your physical eyes. Peter was therefore referring to salvation past. The passage also refers to the trials you're going through now, which serve to prove the genuineness of your faith. This reference relates to salvation present, and it further refers to a coming day when the testing of your faith will result in praise and glory and honor. Here Peter was referring to salvation future.

When does 1 Peter 1:7,13 says you'll receive your future salvation?

At the revelation or revealing or appearing of Jesus, you'll receive your promised inheritance.

In 2 Corinthians 5:1-9 Paul compared our bodies to dwellings or tents. Verses 2 and 4 say we're groaning in our present dwelling. In your opinion, what's the reason for our groaning?

☐ Christians have such hard times in this life.
☐ Christians are terrified of dying.
☐ Christians want to be set free from the old nature.

Verses 2 and 4 make the answer clear, don't they? Paul spoke for all Christians when he spoke of our desire to be free from the physical body with its old nature and all the trials and afflictions the old nature produces. What he longed for is the new body God had prepared for him—one that's perfect because it's free of all the imperfections of the old nature.

Second Corinthians 5:5 should remind you of what you learned from Ephesians 1:13-14 earlier in today's study. What similarity in thought do you see between these two passages?

You see again that you already have the Holy Spirit as a down payment or a guarantee of the future inheritance God has for you.

■ **When you complete this week, you'll have passed the halfway point in your study of *Survival Kit*. Let's do a midpoint checkup.**

How's your daily quiet time developing? You've been studying *Survival Kit* for four weeks. That's thirty-two days, counting weekends. Circle the number of days you've had meaningful times of Bible study, meditation, and prayer.

1	2	3	4	5	6	7
8	9	10	11	12	13	14
15	16	17	18	19	20	21
22	23	24	25	26	27	28
29	30	31	32			

By now you should have memorized four Scripture passages. Can you record them?

Foundation week: Psalm 119:11

Week 1: Romans 12:4-5

Week 2: Galatians 5:16,22-23

Week 3: Philippians 1:6

You should be able to recall three basic truths that have been the themes of weeks 1–3. Record them here as you'd write them on the hand drawing.

One _____

Two _____

Three _____ ____ _____

End your quiet time today by meditating on 1 Peter 1:3-9. Concentrate on discovering what God wants to say to you about salvation future in your life today. Then offer a prayer of committed obedience to God.

Review This Week's Study

This week you examined the three aspects of salvation—beginning, process, and completion. You learned that once you believe in Jesus, nothing can take away the new life you received in Him. You're His forever; He who began a good work in you will surely bring it to completion.

How have memorizing and meditating on Philippians 1:6 this week helped you understand all Jesus has done in saving you?

Summarize each aspect of salvation.

Beginning:

Process:

Completion:

Review the first question on page 97. How does your salvation in Jesus shape the way you live every day?

Why should the completion of your salvation in the future fill you with hope and joy?

FOUR SOURCES OF AUTHORITY

INADEQUATE AND ADEQUATE

Decisions about your spiritual life don't come easily, do they?

Is there a final, ultimate authority you can use to distinguish between what's right and what's wrong, what's good and what's bad? Is there a final, ultimate authority you can depend on as a guide for your daily life?

Yes! That authority isn't experiences, traditions, feelings, or intellect. It's the Bible, God's holy Word. This week you'll learn about that ultimate authority for your life and the way God intends for you to relate experiences, traditions, feelings, and intellect to His Word.

The theme for this week is:

Four Sources of Authority: Inadequate and Adequate

Try labeling the palm, thumb, and next two fingers of the hand drawing. Then label the fourth finger "Four Sources of Authority."

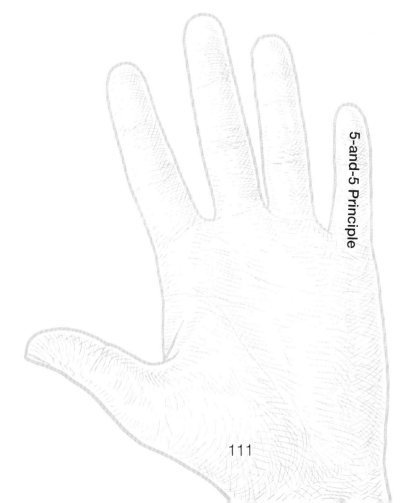

5-and-5 Principle

Three Inadequate Sources

Read Colossians 2:1-4,6-8,20-23.

How many times have you heard or said something like "I want to talk to somebody around here who has a little authority"? How many times have you been told, "I'll have to talk to my manager about that" or "I'm sorry, but I don't have the authority to decide that"? Everybody sometimes feels the need to get in touch with whoever or whatever is the final authority.

All religions and religious systems are based on one or more of four sources of authority. This week you'll learn about three subtle, dangerous sources of authority that others may use as you seek to share your faith with them. These three inadequate sources of authority will also confuse you and distract you in your Christian growth if you don't understand their relationship to the one true source of authority. As you learn about that one true source, you'll recognize how the three inadequate sources relate to it.

The following chart summarizes the four sources of authority. Take each heading in the boxes above the chart and record it above the description you think fits it best. You can find an answer key on page 115.

EXPERIENCES	INTELLECT	SCRIPTURE	TRADITION
Sources inside Yourself		**Sources outside Yourself**	
_____ You determine truth by your ability to reason and conclude what's right or wrong, good or bad.		_____ You structure your beliefs by those that have been important to your ancestors.	
_____ You determine truth by your senses, feelings, and emotions.		_____ God reveals His truth in written form. That truth is your final, ultimate authority.	

The apostle Paul knew a great deal about inadequate sources of authority. In his missionary journeys he found many people who depended on those inadequate sources rather than the one true source of authority. He wrote many of his letters to oppose leaders who were promoting inadequate sources of authority and to urge Christians to hold to the one true source.

■ **Read Colossians 2:1-4.**

In verse 2 Paul said he wanted the Colossian Christians to be wealthy. What kind of wealth was he talking about?

Paul wanted the Colossian Christians to have complete or full assurance of understanding.

In verse 3 Paul told them they would find a twofold treasure hidden in Christ Himself. What was that treasure?

_____ and _____

Why did Paul want his fellow believers to have this treasure? Verse 4 tells you.

We need to pay attention to what Paul said in Colossians 2:8 because we're all in danger of being misled or of forming incorrect ideas:

> Be careful that no one takes you captive through philosophy
> and empty deceit based on human tradition, based
> on the elements of the world, rather than Christ.
> **COLOSSIANS 2:8**

In this verse Paul clearly identified one of the inadequate sources of authority, and he clearly implied another. Which did he clearly identify?

☐ Experience   ☐ Intellect   ☐ Tradition

Which did he clearly imply?

☐ Experience   ☐ Intellect   ☐ Tradition

Did you check *tradition* as the inadequate source Paul clearly identified? You should have checked *intellect* as the one he clearly implied. The appeal of philosophy is to the mind and reasoning processes—that is, the intellect. Paul said the false philosophers were engaging in meaningless deception. That deception was to mislead the thoughts and ideas of people who listened to them.

What did Paul mean when he said you could be taken captive by these wrong sources of authority? Look again at verse 4.

Have you ever met anyone whose mind was so captivated by a false idea that he couldn't even understand what you were trying to say? That's the type of deception Paul was talking about.

Your first Scripture-memory assignment for this week is 1 Corinthians 2:14. Later this week you'll study this verse in more detail. Begin now to memorize it.

■ **Read Colossians 2:20-23.**

What powerful argument did Paul give against your living in accordance with "human commands and doctrines" (verse 22)? Note the first part of verse 20.

Intellect, tradition, and experiences are human standards. Paul argued that you shouldn't live by mere human standards because you've died with Christ. Colossians 2:23 says these human standards can appear to be wise and appropriate, but they're forever destined to be inadequate and unfit when they aren't subject to the one true source of authority—Jesus Christ.

God gave you your mind, your intellect; He expects you to use it. God gives you experiences; He expects you to consider them. Some principles and practices are unchanging, regardless of passing centuries. Some traditions—especially those based on Scripture—are worth preserving. But neither intellect, experiences, nor tradition should become your ultimate authority for faith.

After looking more closely at the three inadequate sources, we'll see how that the Bible, God's Word, is the ultimate, accurate, sufficient source of authority because it's the record of who Jesus was, what He taught, and what He did.

Experiences, intellect, and tradition can help us discover and understand truth only when they're understood and interpreted in light of what the Bible teaches.

End your quiet time today by meditating on Colossians 2:6-8. How should this passage influence what you believe, how you feel, or the way you behave? What will you promise God you'll do about it?

You should have arranged the titles on the chart on page 112 like this:

Intellect	Tradition
Experiences	Scripture

Intellect and Tradition

Read Mark 12:18-25; 1 Corinthians 1:18-25; 2:7-14; Matthew 15:1-9; 1 Peter 1:18-19.

Our determination to use intellect and logic as our final authority is the way we most clearly crown ourselves the god of our lives. On the other hand, our dependence on tradition and ritual is the way we most clearly escape responsibility for making decisions and being accountable for them. Let's look at these two sources of authority to see why alone they're inadequate.

Something about the human race makes us believe we can make judgments about truth and error, good and evil, right and wrong, using no more than our intellect. Nevertheless, all of history gives evidence that we continually use poor judgment and that intellect alone isn't adequate to make moral and spiritual decisions.

Yet people still refuse to believe Scripture and trust Christ because they can't reach Him through their intellect. They say, "I just can't understand how a good God could …" or "It's not reasonable to believe that God would …"

◼ **During His earthly ministry Jesus had to deal with this kind of thinking. Read Mark 12:18-25.**

The Sadducees were a major group of Jewish religious leaders in Jesus' day. According to verse 18, what did the Sadducees refuse to believe?

To support their intellectual doubts about resurrection after death, the Sadducees told Jesus a long story. Check what you think was the basis of their story.

☐ The teaching of Scripture
☐ Their own reasoning

In verse 24 how did Jesus analyze the Sadducees' reasoning?

Jesus said they were _____ because they knew neither

the _____ nor the _____ ____ _____.

The Sadducees were mistaken (or wrong or in error) because they understood neither the Scriptures nor the power of God.

Do you think the Sadducees were really searching for truth when they came to Jesus?

Yes   No

What was the Sadducees' source of authority for their religious system?

■ **Like Jesus, Paul had to cope with people who made intellect the source of authority for their beliefs. Read 1 Corinthians 1:18-25.**

A word in verse 20 well describes the Sadducees who came to Jesus. Record the word here.

Trying to debate or dispute with people about what they believe rarely does any good. Paul even said in verses 20-21 that God has made foolishness of what the world considers wisdom. And the world considers foolishness the truth that leads to salvation.

Paul analyzed the way the two major ethnic groups of his day used the wisdom of the world:

The Jews ask for signs and the Greeks seek wisdom, but we preach Christ crucified, a stumbling block to the Jews and foolishness to the Gentiles. Yet to those who are called, both Jews and Greeks, Christ is the power of God and the wisdom of God, because God's foolishness is wiser than human wisdom, and God's weakness is stronger than human strength.
1 CORINTHIANS 1:22-25

These verses don't mean the Christian faith is anti-intellectual—far from it! Paul himself had one of the most brilliant and highly educated minds of his century.

> Read 1 Corinthians 2:7-8 to learn what kind of wisdom Paul taught. He said if earthly rulers had understood this true wisdom, they wouldn't have committed what terrible crime?

Paul didn't accuse humankind of having too much wisdom but of having too little of the right kind of wisdom. If they had enough true wisdom, they wouldn't have crucified the Lord Jesus Christ.

> Now read 1 Corinthians 2:9-11 to learn why people of the world didn't understand who Jesus was or why He came. According to verse 11, who's the only person who understands God's thoughts?

> If only the Spirit of God understands the thoughts of God, what's the only way people can understand them? Read verses 12-13 to find out. Summarize those verses in your own words.

Did you write something like this? Christians have received the Spirit of God, who teaches us God's truth.

> According to 1 Corinthians 2:14, why is it impossible for us to find God through our intellect?

A natural, worldly person (anyone whose life isn't committed to Christ) hasn't received the Spirit of God. According to that same verse, you can't depend on reason alone when you talk with a person who holds intellect as the ultimate authority. You must ask God to use His Holy Spirit to create the kind of awareness and conviction that will prepare a person to believe.

> *You should have found 1 Corinthians 2:14 familiar when*
> *you read it today. Try recording it from memory. Then*
> *use your Scripture-memory card to check your recall.*

Now let's consider why tradition alone is also an inadequate source of authority. Traditions usually develop when someone in the past decided a particular teaching, custom, or ceremony should be repeated again and again. For that person, the teaching, custom, or ceremony was so important that it must be preserved and not forgotten.

Often, however, the deep heart meaning of the teaching, custom, or ceremony has been lost. Only the form remains and continues to be observed as no more than ritual that calls for no real heart commitment. Tradition can become a jail cell, imprisoning people who might find the true meaning of the original teaching, custom, or ceremony if it were expressed another way.

The religious leaders were critical of Jesus' disciples because they didn't wash their hands a certain way before eating. But Jesus said these religious leaders were ignoring a more important matter.

■ Read Matthew 15:1-9.

Which of the Ten Commandments did Jesus accuse the religious leaders of breaking?

The Pharisees and scribes were breaking the commandment to honor their fathers and mothers.

When it comes to Scripture versus tradition, you must make a clear-cut choice. Summarize in your own words Isaiah's prophecy quoted by Jesus in Matthew 15:8-9.

Some people give God lip service instead of heart service.

Read 1 Peter 1:18-19. According to those verses, can tradition bring salvation to people? In light of the verses from Matthew that you studied today, why not?

Did you write that tradition tends to become a matter of outward expression, not of the heart, and that human traditions sometimes contradict God's Word?

Do you know people who've been misled by their intellect or who are trapped by religious tradition? List a few and commit to pray for them by name during your quiet time.

Experience

Read Deuteronomy 13:1-4; Colossians 2:18-19; 2 Peter 1:16-21.

From the beginning of time, people have used personal experiences as the basis of their religious beliefs and have considered anyone else who hadn't had the same kind of experience to be spiritually inferior or substandard. Using nothing more than experience as the basis for your beliefs is dangerous. God uses a better way to reveal Himself. He has given us a written record of truth. All the experiences of life must be judged by that record.

■ Read Deuteronomy 13:1-4.

According to these verses, check which statement is a more reliable test of truth in the experience of a prophet or a dreamer.

☐ Whether the prophecy or dream comes true
☐ Whether the prophet or dreamer entices you
  to turn away from the one true God

Even when people can show you signs and wonders and their predictions seem accurate, you mustn't listen to them if they diminish your single-hearted devotion to God.

What reason does Deuteronomy 13:3 give that people who make experiences their religious authority sometimes seem so persuasive?

God may permit a person to speak persuasively with what seems to be great authority. That person may even claim a special relationship with God and perform miracles. God permits these abilities and claims in order to give you an opportunity to demonstrate your love and commitment to Him. He also permits situations to be created that require you to flex your spiritual muscles and grow spiritually.

■ **Clinging to experiences as the source of religious authority always causes problems. Read Colossians 2:18-19.**

What specific problem was the apostle Paul writing about?

Some of the Colossians had apparently seen visions. As a result, they were trying to persuade all of the other Christians to join in the worship of angels and other false practices.

According to verse 19, what's the mistake people make when they use experiences as their authority?

According to verse 19, what's the source of growth in the body of Christ?

Paul said people who hold to experiences as their authority don't hold fast to Christ, the Head of His body, the church. Basing their faith on a special or unusual experience, they often consider themselves spiritually superior to others who haven't had the same experience.

Without a doubt, your deepening fellowship with God will produce deeply significant experiences in your life. Those experiences can be a blessing to you and to other Christians. But beware of insisting that others have the same kind of experience. And beware of others who insist that you try to have the same experience they've had.

When Christians begin seeking an experience
instead of fellowship with God, they're in danger
of being captured by a false source of authority.

Experiences, like intellect and tradition, must be interpreted in light of Scripture. Read 2 Peter 1:16-18. In this passage Peter described Jesus' transfiguration, a remarkable event he had seen with his own eyes. Peter made these statements about the experience:

- "We were eyewitnesses of his majesty" (verse 16).
- "He received honor and glory from God the Father" (verse 17).
- "The voice came to him, … saying, 'This is my beloved Son, with whom I am well-pleased!' " (verse 17).
- "We ourselves heard this voice when it came from heaven" (verse 18).
- "We were with him on the holy mountain" (verse 18).

Now read an actual written account of the event recorded in Matthew 17:1-5. Check off each of Peter's statements that the actual account verifies.

It's clear that Peter knew what he was talking about, isn't it? But carefully read what Peter said next in 2 Peter 1:19-21.

Did you notice that he spoke of something being "strongly confirmed" (verse 19)? What could be more sure than something he had seen with his own eyes? You might say, "Nothing could be more certain that!" Yet Peter said, "We also have the prophetic word strongly confirmed" (verse 19). Peter was identifying something even more trustworthy than what he saw and heard himself: words written by the prophets, who had been guided by the Holy Spirit of God.

Beginning this week, you'll have two Scripture-memory assignments. The first Scripture speaks about people who are depending on any of the three inadequate sources of authority. By now you should be able to record 1 Corinthians 2:14 from memory. See if you can. Then use your Scripture-memory card to check your recall.

Tomorrow you'll begin learning about the one true, ultimate source of authority. Your second Scripture-memory assignment addresses that source. Begin memorizing 2 Timothy 3:16 now.

Let's summarize what we've learned about the three inadequate sources of authority: intellect, tradition, and experiences. Separately or together these three sources of religious authority never rise above the best people can do when they have no truth from God. Because all of these are based on human structures, they're all dead-end streets.

The frequently heard proposition that all religions lead to the same God simply isn't true. A person who makes such a statement has never studied all religions. Indeed, some religions don't even admit that God exists.

If you haven't already heard sincere, earnest people present different religious claims and teaching, you will. They may sincerely try to sway you to their beliefs. Carefully examine their claims. Are they based on intellect? The human mind can't be the final judge of spiritual truth. Are they based on experience? Human activities can't be the final source for spiritual truth. Are they based on tradition? Our past intellect and experiences are no more trustworthy than our present ones.

■ **Read 1 Timothy 1:3-7.**

According to verse 4, what do human teachings lead to?

Mere speculations, questions, or arguments do nothing to strengthen you as a Christian. On the other hand, where does true teaching from God lead? True teaching from God leads to a pure heart, a good conscience, and sincere faith.

In 2 Timothy 2:18 Paul pointed out that false teachings had upset or overthrown the faith of some people. According to verse 19, what did Paul identify that would enable Timothy to stand firm?

The firm foundation of teaching from the Word of God stood as strong as ever.

Conclude your quiet time today by meditating on 2 Peter 1:16-21. Wait before God and let Him reveal how those verses should affect the way you live your life today.

Scripture: The One True Source, Part 1

Read Isaiah 53:5,7,9; 2 Timothy 1:2-5; 3:14-17.

The Bible is truly an amazing book. It contains hundreds of statements about events that hadn't yet happened when the authors wrote about them but later came to pass. Prophecies about future kings and kingdoms, predictions of births and deaths, forecasts of the Savior's coming into the world—all are found in the Bible. Let's look at an example.

■ **Read Micah 5:2; then read Matthew 2:1-6.**

Where did the prophet Micah say the Savior was to be born?

Where was Jesus born?

Next read the following passage. It's part of a marvelous prophetic poem Isaiah wrote. I've marked subdivisions of the verses.

> 5a He was pierced because of our rebellion,
> 5b crushed because of our iniquities;
> 5c punishment for our peace was on him,
> 5d and we are healed by his wounds.
> 7a He was oppressed and afflicted,
> 7b yet He did not open His mouth.
> 9a He was assigned a grave with the wicked,
> 9b but he was with a rich man at his death,
> 9c because he had done no violence
> 9d and had not spoken deceitfully.
> **ISAIAH 53:5,7,9**

Now read the following New Testament verses. Beside each one, record the number and letter of one or more verse subdivisions from Isaiah 53. I've completed the first one for you. Answers are at the end of this day's study.

   5a John 19:34   ____ Matthew 27:14
   ____ John 20:25   ____ Matthew 27:38
   ____ John 19:1   ____ Matthew 27:57-60
   ____ Matthew 27:13   ____ John 19:4

Isaiah 53 was written hundreds of years before Christ was born? In those days execution on the cross was totally unknown. Yet the word *pierced* in verse 5 described both the use of nails in Jesus' crucifixion and the sword wound in His side. How could anyone have guessed that Jesus would be assigned for execution "with the wicked" (verse 9; the two robbers on the crosses on each side) and yet end up "with a rich man at his death" (verse 9; Joseph of Arimathea, who buried Him)? Only the Spirit of God could have given the prophet these facts.

Our Lord Jesus Himself made predictions of the future; read one in John 14:2-3. What two future events did Jesus prophesy?

    1.

    2.

Jesus predicted (1) that He would prepare a place for you in heaven and (2) that He would come again and take you to be with Him in that place.

What reason do you have to believe Jesus will keep these promises in the future?

Many Bible prophecies have already come true. For that reason you can be confident that the others will eventually be fulfilled as well. The Bible is filled with predictions. Only God could have made each one, without exception, totally accurate. Isn't God's Word an amazing book?

Four sources of authority, but only one is trustworthy!

The apostle Paul knew which one that source was.

■ **Read 2 Timothy 3:14-17.**

> **Focus on verse 15. How long had Timothy been studying the Scriptures?**

> **Because Timothy had studied the Scriptures ever since he was a child, what did he know the Scriptures were able to give him?**

What other writings in all the world can give you the kind of wisdom that will lead you to "salvation through faith in Christ Jesus"? None!

> **Now focus on verse 14. What did Paul instruct young Timothy to do?**

> **What's the difference between learning a truth and firmly believing that truth?**

> **Focus now on 2 Timothy 3:16. This is your second Scripture-memory assignment for this week, so you should know what it says without referring to your Bible. Because the Bible was given to us by God's inspiration, for what four purposes is it useful?**

>> 1.
>>
>> 2.
>>
>> 3.
>>
>> 4.

Let's be sure you understand what verse 16 means when it uses the word *inspired* to describe the Scriptures. The root word means "to breathe into." Scripture is the direct work of God, who breathed His truth into the minds of the people who wrote the Bible.

The Bible doesn't just contain truth; the Bible is truth. It's the ultimate, supreme record of God's truth.

Although other sources may be helpful, none are essential—whether they're books, visions, experiences, or traditions.

The Scriptures, are useful "for teaching, for rebuking, for correcting, for training in righteousness." Studying them will have an obvious effect on your life.

Focus now on verse 17. What will you become as you study the Scriptures?

Do you really want to become "complete, equipped for every good work"? If you do, you know how. You're doing it now if you're being faithful to read the Bible and meditate on it during your quiet time, working through daily studies in your *Survival Kit,* and learning your Scripture-memory verses.

Your first Scripture-memory assignment in this study, Psalm 119:11, gives the reason memorizing God's Word is so important. If you're regularly reviewing your memory assignments, you should be able to record that verse here from memory.

Timothy had been studying the Scriptures since he was a child. You can't begin a lifetime of study any sooner than today. End your quiet time today with this prayer commitment:

For the rest of my life, I will give priority time to reading, studying, and meditating on God's holy Scriptures.

Answers to Scripture-matching exercise on page 126: 5a—John 19:34; 7b—Matthew 27:14; 5a—John 20:25; 9a—Matthew 27:38; 5d—John 19:1; 9b—Matthew 27:57–60; 7a—Matthew 27:13; 9c, 9d—John 19:4

DAY 5

Scripture:
The One True Source, Part 2

Read 1 Corinthians 15:3-7; Acts 18:24,28; Hebrews 5:12-14.

In the verses you'll study today, you'll find many different expressions for the Word of God, such as law, precepts, testimonies, statutes, commandments, and judgments. In the Bible the expression "Word of God" also has a broader meaning than the Bible alone. It means anything God says about Himself, whether through the voice of His prophet, through the majesty of His creation, or through the ordering of human history in His world. "Word of God" refers to the active expression of God's very nature. As such, it certainly includes the Scriptures—writings that are the unique record of God's activity.

The Bible claims to be an eternal source of wisdom and righteousness.

■ **Carefully read each of the following verses: Psalm 19:7-11; 37:29-31; 119:89-91,98-101,130,160; Isaiah 40:6-8.**

These verses focus on the great claims the Bible makes for itself: that it's eternal or everlasting, a source of wisdom, and a source of righteousness. Beside each of the following key words, write the reference of each verse in which the Bible makes that claim for itself.

Eternal:
Wisdom:
Righteousness:

In addition to the verses you just read, your second Scripture-memory assignment for this week is a passage in which the Bible makes a claim for itself. Can you quote 2 Timothy 3:16 here?

Another verse you've learned explains why many people misunderstand the Bible. The Bible was inspired by the Spirit of God and can be rightly interpreted only by people who are indwelled by the Spirit of God.

Write 1 Corinthians 2:14 here.

Where does Psalm 37:31 say the authority of the Scriptures should be kept?

Isn't it comforting to know that when you have God's Word in your heart, your steps on the pathway of life won't slip or falter? Four sources of authority, but only one of them is trustworthy. You know which one that is.

■ **The apostle Paul also knew which source of authority is trustworthy. Read what Paul wrote in 1 Corinthians 15:3-8.**

Twice Paul mentioned the authority he was using for his summary of the death, burial, and resurrection of Jesus Christ. Which source of authority was it?

You too can use the Scriptures as your source of authority when you share Christ with others. But this doesn't come naturally to you even though you're a Christian.

■ **Read in Acts 18:24,28 a capsule biography of a Christian named Apollos.**

How do you think Apollos became so skilled in his knowledge and use of Scripture?

Is it important for you to know the Scriptures as well as Apollos knew them? Is it important enough to rearrange your personal priorities in order to study the Scriptures? What areas of your life might have to be rearranged to provide the time you need for a lifelong habit of Bible study?

In all honesty are you ready and willing to rearrange your priorities at this time?

Yes   No

■ **Read again Acts 18:28.**

What did Apollos have to do before he was capable of publicly demonstrating that Jesus was the Messiah, the Christ?

Would you like to be able to share Christ openly?

Yes   No

If so, what steps could you take now to prepare yourself as Apollos did?

■ **Read Hebrews 5:12-14.**

According to these verses, what was the tragic result when some Christians never bothered to develop personal Bible-study habits?

How tragic when Christians who should be mature enough to serve as teachers still need someone to teach them the basics of God's Word! Such people are just the opposite of Apollos, aren't they?

List the names of one or two people who remind you of Apollos and one or two who remind you of the Christians described in Hebrews 5:12-14.

If someone else were making the list, where would your name appear?

Although God has given you an intellect, He didn't intend for it to become the final authority to determine right and wrong, good and bad. Your intellect is simply an instrument for you to use in seeking God's guidance.

Although you'll have significant experiences with God, these are never to be worshiped or exalted. They're simply the by-products of your wonderful fellowship with Him. Experiences may fade away as time passes, but "Jesus Christ is the same yesterday, today, and forever" (Hebrews 13:8). You must never let a preoccupation with an experience replace your fellowship with Him.

Some traditions, like intellect and experiences, may be rooted in God's will and purpose. However, when you do things from ritual and habit without understanding or believing in their value, you're in the prison of tradition. Only the blood of Christ can set you free. He has come to give you reality, not mere formalism. A firsthand relationship with Christ is better than a tradition that has been handed down from your forefathers.

And so you come back to Scripture, your final and perfect authority.

Isn't it great to know the Bible contains all you need to know about your faith and your life as a Christian?

Because this is true, no part of your life as a Christian should be more important than your study of the Scriptures.

Pastors proclaim the Scriptures and teachers explain the Scriptures because they believe the final and perfect authority of the Bible. You'll profit from their preaching and teaching. Yet there's an even more important relationship you can have with your Bible—a personal relationship.

Review the responses you made earlier in today's work. What did you say you needed to do now to prepare yourself to share Christ effectively? What adjustments did you say you must make to cultivate a lifetime habit of Bible study? End your quiet time with a prayer in which you commit to follow up on those priorities.

Review This Week's Study

Explain in your own words why each of these sources of authority is inadequate.

Experiences, feelings, emotions:

Tradition:

Intellect:

The daily commitments at the end of your quiet-time exercises this week encouraged you to make decisions and commitments that could be life-changing. Summarize the most significant decision or commitment you made and ways you expect it to affect your life as a Christian.

THE FIVE-AND-FIVE PRINCIPLE

REACHING OTHERS THROUGH PRAYER AND WITNESSING

Multitudes of Christians sleep in the silent-Christian stage. Don't be one of them!

Christ has commanded us to share the gospel with lost people. Christians who don't verbally witness may be busy in the church, but they usually aren't very effective in bringing other people to faith in Christ. The kind of witnessing that produces results is the witness of a Christ-indwelled life working together with your verbal testimony.

The theme for this week is:

The Five-and-Five Principle: Reaching Others through Prayer and Witnessing

The five-and-five principle is a simple, practical approach to witnessing to your lost friends. If you master and apply the five-and-five principle, I can guarantee that you'll increase the effectiveness with which you obey your Lord's command to share the gospel. And you'll realize an even greater sense of joy and fulfillment as you do so.

Ten You Can Win

Read Philippians 4:6; 1 Timothy 2:1,3-4,8.

Look at your left hand. Use the fingers on that hand to count five people in your life who won't permit you to share your faith with them. They may be cold, skeptical, suspicious, unconcerned, or even hostile toward what you would like to tell them about Christ and what He has done and is doing for you. Although you want to share your faith with them so that they can also become Christians, they aren't willing to hear what you want to say.

Is there anything you can do that will enable you to reach them with the message of Christ? Yes! You can pray for them!

Look at your right hand. Count on those fingers five people in your life who will permit you to share your faith with them. They may not be ready to place their faith in Christ, but they recognize the difference Christ is making in your life.

Is there something you can do to bring them to trust Christ? Yes! You can pray for them and share your faith with them!

Let's spend today laying the foundation for the five-and-five principle in your life. You've already identified ten people you can win. Now you must understand the importance of prayer in winning both those who will listen to you and those who won't.

The power of prayer is even more important than the act of witnessing because prayer power works with both those who will and those who won't let you share Christ with them. A great Christian once said, "You can do more than pray after you've prayed, but you can do no more than pray—until you've prayed!"

Philippians 4:6 is your first Scripture-memory assignment for this week. You should begin memorizing it now. (If you're using the King James Version, substitute anxious *for the word* careful.*)*

According to this verse, what's the alternative to being anxious about any or all of the situations you face in life?

What limits does this verse put on matters you can pray about?

A Christian can talk to God in prayer about everything. What is prayer anyhow?

Prayer is letting Christ use His power to work in an area of need in your life or in the life of another person.

Prayer is your invitation to Christ to come into an area of need. The answer to your prayer doesn't depend on your power in prayer but on His power to work in that area of need. Therefore, praying for your unbelieving friends who won't permit you to share your faith with them is simply inviting Christ to work in their lives in spite of their attitude toward you.

■ **Read 1 Timothy 2:1.**

In this verse the apostle Paul urged that prayer be made for whom?

Praying for all people may seem rather broad and general. Let's say it another way. You should feel no hesitation to pray for anyone, regardless of that person's position, circumstances, or attitude.

In 1 Timothy 2:4 Paul specified two reasons God wants you to pray. What are they?

1.

2.

If God wants everyone to be saved and to know the truth, you should understand the way God wants to make it happen.

In 1 Timothy 2:8 the apostle Paul, speaking for God, stated one more thing God wants. What is it?

The mention of "lifting up holy hands" refers to the way people normally prayed during New Testament times. They normally didn't kneel or bow as we do. Instead, they stood looking toward heaven with hands lifted. You too can pray standing with your hands lifted toward heaven. Or you can kneel to pray, be seated to pray, or even pray while you're engaged in another activity.

> **The point Paul was making has nothing to do with the posture we assume to pray. So what do you think Paul was saying God expects of us in regard to prayer?**

A key word in 1 Timothy 2:8 is *holy*. Do you remember from one of your first studies in *Survival Kit* that *holy* means "set apart" or "dedicated to a special purpose"? First of all, God want us to be committed to prayer. Prayer should be a natural, consistent part of your daily life.

The second key to praying effectively is to be free of "anger or argument." We can't expect to be on good speaking terms with God if we're not on good speaking terms with one another. Wrong attitudes and wrong feelings make a difference in the power of our prayers.

■ **Read Matthew 5:23-24.**

> **What did Jesus say about the relationship between our access to God and our relationships with fellow Christians?**

Think again about your first Scripture-memory assignment for this week. I hope you'll do more than just learn it. Begin right now to practice it. Let me suggest a way.

■ **List the names of the ten persons you identified at the beginning of today's study.**

Friends who refuse to let me share Christ with them:

1. _____

2. _____

3. _____

4. _____

5. _____

Friends who are open to my sharing Christ:

1. _____

2. _____

3. _____

4. _____

5. _____

Now meditate on 1 Timothy 2:8. Do you need to make any changes before you can bring the power of prayer to bear on these friends you want to be saved?

End your quiet time with a prayer of commitment to make those changes with God's help. Then pray for each person you listed. Call each one by name and invite Christ to begin working in their lives.

DAY 2

Five You Can Only Pray For

Read Matthew 7:7-11; 17:20; 21:21-22; James 1:5-8; John 6:37.

Yesterday you used the fingers of your left hand to identify five people who won't let you share your faith with them. These are people for whom you can only pray. Then you used the fingers of your right hand to identify five people who will let you share your faith with them. These are persons you can both pray for and witness to.

■ Read Matthew 21:21-22 and James 1:5-8.

In light of these verses, do you tend to feel discouraged, hesitant, or afraid when you think about praying for your lost friends to be saved? If so, why do you feel that way?

The reason you feel hesitant or afraid to pray for your friends is important. Are you afraid your faith may not be strong enough or that you won't get an answer to those prayers for another reason?

Read John 6:37 and think again about praying for those lost friends. How much faith must you have before Jesus will answer your prayers? Find the answer in Matthew 17:20.

Jesus said even faith as small as a mustard seed is enough. If your faith is strong enough to bring you to Jesus with your need, it's enough. He has promised that He will honor such faith. He will "never cast out" (John 6:37) anyone who trusts Him.

If you have enough faith to come to Jesus with your inability to help yourself, He will deal with your doubts. Don't feel your faith is so weak that praying would do no good. Remember, prayer is simply letting Christ use His power to work in an area of need—in your life or in the life of another person.

If your faith in Jesus is large enough to ask Him to use His power and reveal Himself to your five-and-five people, it's large enough.

Your faith is never stronger than when you admit your lack of power and you trust Jesus to use His limitless power.

So never think your imperfect faith can place a limit on His power. Pray! It's as simple as giving your Lord access to an area of need. Just let yourself go during your prayer times and do what Philippians 4:6 encourages you to do.

Have you memorized that verse yet? Try to record it here from memory.

At the end of this quiet time, I'll ask you to pray for the first five of the five-and-five you listed yesterday. First let's look at three aspects of prayer that will help you as you pray.

■ **Read Matthew 7:7-8.**

Often we describe prayer as talking with God. These verses describe praying as three different actions. Each action brings a specific result. List the actions and the accompanying results.

ACTION	RESULT
1.	
2.	
3.	

Did you find it easy to identify the right answers? Now meditate on the three verbs or actions used in Matthew 7:7-8.

Asking in prayer involves requesting something you already know about: "Lord Jesus, I ask You to bring my friend to know Your love." You already know about Christ's love; you simply want your unbelieving friend to trust Christ and come to know that love as you know it.

Seeking in prayer, on the other hand, involves requesting an answer about something you don't know about: "Lord Jesus, show me what I can do to express Your love to my friend. I don't know what to do next."

Knocking in prayer involves asking Christ to enter an area of need that's behind closed doors: "Lord Jesus, deep immorality in my friend's life has closed him to Your love. Open the door to that area of need in him and show him that You can deliver him."

■ **Read Matthew 7:9-11.**

> **These verses make several comparisons. Which comparison is most important?**

The most important comparison in Matthew 7:9-11 doesn't involve bread or stone, a fish or a snake. Rather, it's the comparison between a human father's integrity and compassion and the integrity and compassion of your Heavenly Father.

> **What assurance do these verses give you that asking, seeking, and knocking in prayer will be answered?**

If human fathers give what their children ask for, we can certainly expect our Heavenly Father to give us what we ask for.

> **Do you agree that this is a fair summary of the teaching in Matthew 7:9-11?**

> **What are you asking your Heavenly Father to give you when you pray for your first five lost friends? Be practical.**

You're asking your Heavenly Father to bring salvation to the five people for whom you can only pray because they're not open to your sharing Christ with them.

Briefly review the three aspects of prayer I explained earlier. What can you ask, seek, or knock for when you pray for those five people today?

1. Name: _____

    Ask: _____

    Seek: _____

    Knock: _____

2. Name: _____

    Ask: _____

    Seek: _____

    Knock: _____

3. Name: _____

    Ask: _____

    Seek: _____

    Knock: _____

4. Name: _____

    Ask: _____

    Seek: _____

    Knock: _____

5. Name: _____

    Ask: _____

    Seek: _____

    Knock: _____

The only way you'll discover the power of prayer in reaching the seeming unreachables in your life is to pray for them.

End your quiet time today by asking, seeking, and knocking for each one. Pray about a specific area of need in each life. Commit yourself to pray each day. Then wait for the results of your prayers. God has His own timetable for answering—and He will answer!

Three Aspects of Prayer

Read Matthew 28:18-20; 14:23; Mark 1:35; Luke 6:12; 22:39-41; John 14:13-14.

The apostle Paul knew prayer is important. Philippians 4:6 proves it.

Can you write Philippians 4:6 from memory?

Prayer is a faith exercise. Yesterday you studied something Jesus said that showed the importance of prayer.

Can you summarize Matthew 21:21-22 in one sentence? If you don't remember, check the work you did yesterday.

Now read Matthew 14:23; Mark 1:35; Luke 6:12; 22:39-41. According to these verses, where are three places Jesus went to pray?

　　1.

　　2.

　　3.

Prayer is being with God. Jesus prayed in the hills, at a lonely or solitary place, and on the Mount of Olives. He prayed at night and at early morning before daybreak.

Why do you think Jesus chose such times and places for prayer?

Luke 22:41 should have given you a clue to the answer. Jesus withdrew "about a stone's throw" from His disciples. He chose times and places when He could be alone with the Father.

> **What words in which of the verses you read tell you that prayer was a lifetime habit for Jesus?**

> **Did you spot the words "as usual" in Luke 22:39? Which verse tells you how long Jesus sometimes prayed?**

Prayer is a life pattern. Luke 6:12 tells you that Jesus sometimes prayed all night long. Think what this means. Jesus lived in constant prayer fellowship with God the Father. Nevertheless, Jesus found it necessary to withdraw from the pressures of life at regular times and at special places in order to pray. Sometimes He prayed for hours at a time.

> **In light of Jesus' habit of prayer, what conclusion can you draw about your prayer life?**

Growing in Christ is essentially a matter of getting your priorities in order.

Prayer is a priority. Before you gave the indwelling Christ complete control, you did many things that are now low-priority items in your life. Because old habits still trap you, you may need to deliberately restructure your time to make time for prayer.

> **When and where do you—or will you—go to pray specifically for your unsaved friends?**

■ **Yesterday you studied what Jesus said in Matthew 7:7-8 about asking, seeking, and knocking. Now read what He said in John 14:13-14.**

Each of those verses tells you to ask in a certain way as you pray. In whose name are you to pray?

When you make your request in the name of Jesus, whose glorious power is released to work?

God the Father, who is all-powerful, will be glorified in Christ the Son as you pray in Jesus' name. Prayer is trusting Christ's power.

■ **Now read Matthew 28:18-20.**

According to verse 18, how much power is released by praying in the name of Jesus?

"All authority has been given to me in heaven and on earth." What an awesome statement! And what awesome power is at your disposal when you pray in Jesus' name!

Learn a lesson of the five-and-five principle. You've probably found praying for the five who are open to your sharing easier than praying for the five who aren't open. Is it because the five who aren't open to you are harder to reach?

Wait! You must reject such an idea. Remember, Christ is the One who's reaching them. What you think is hard or easy looks completely different to God. Thinking one person is harder to reach than another person only limits your prayer life. When you pray in the name of Jesus for those friends, the One you're inviting to enter their lives has all power in heaven and on earth.

Does it matter to a tornado sweeping through a forest that some trees are hardwood and others are softwood? Of course not! The tornado's power is vastly greater than either softwood or hardwood.

Don't underestimate the power of your prayers.
When you ask the Lord to enter a life, never
doubt His ability to do what you ask.

God can do more than you ask or think (see Ephesians 3:20). All the power in the universe rests in His name.

Before ending your quiet time today, see if you can fill in all of the words that should be on the hand drawing. Use page 6 to check your work.

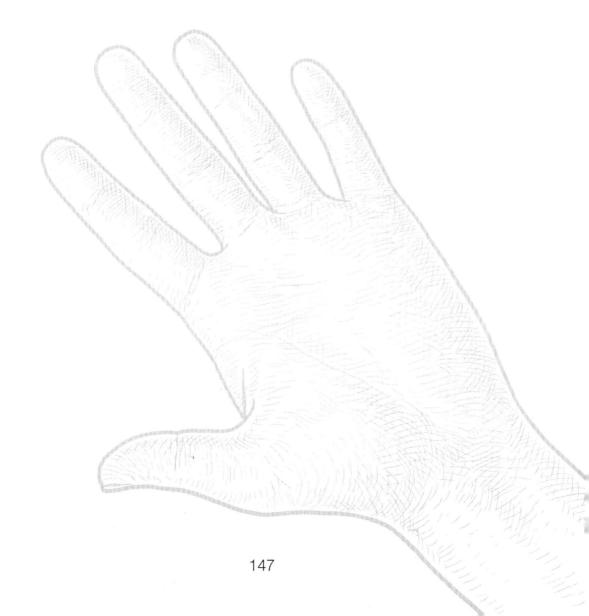

Praying for your lost friends puts the power of God to work in their lives. Nothing you do could possibly be more important than that.

> What could you eliminate, readjust, or cancel in your weekly schedule that would allow you to have a special time and place to pray for your lost friends?

> How much time will you need to ask, seek, and knock for each of those friends?

> Will you combine praying for these friends with your regular quiet time, or will you set a different time to pray for them? When and where will you pray for these friends?

> End your quiet time today with a commitment to make time to pray for your lost friends.

Five You Can Witness To

Read Acts 1:8; John 15:26-27.

For the rest of your life, keep the ten fingers of your two hands full. As long as you serve Christ, always have five people you're praying for and five people you're witnessing to.

The basic meaning of the word *witness* is "one who furnishes evidence." Witnessing isn't preaching. It's not even teaching the Bible. It's giving evidence. You believe in Christ as your Savior and Lord, and He lives in your life. As a result, your personality has an added ingredient that's evident to the people around you. That added ingredient is Christ, causing His love to flow through you.

Jesus was talking with His followers shortly before returning to heaven. He made a great claim, gave a great command, and made a great promise. All three are found in Matthew 28:18-20.

> *Matthew 28:18-20 is your second Scripture-memory assignment for this week. Record it here and begin memorizing it now.*

Underline the great claim Jesus made. You studied this claim yesterday when you learned about the great power of prayer.

Now circle the great promise Jesus made in the last part of those verses. Everything in between is the great command He gave all His followers. It's usually called the Great Commission.

■ **In Acts 1:8 you can find another important promise and command Jesus gave to His followers shortly before ending His earthly ministry. Read that verse now.**

According to Jesus, what must happen before Christians begin witnessing?

Why is it necessary for Jesus' followers to receive the Holy Spirit?

In Acts 1:8 Jesus named geographical areas in which His followers were to be witnesses in the power of the Holy Spirit. He started with Jerusalem, the city where they were at that moment. Then He moved out to more distant areas.

Look at the four circles in the drawing on the left. The innermost circle has already been filled in. Fill in the other circles, moving outward according to the instruction Jesus gave in Acts 1:8.

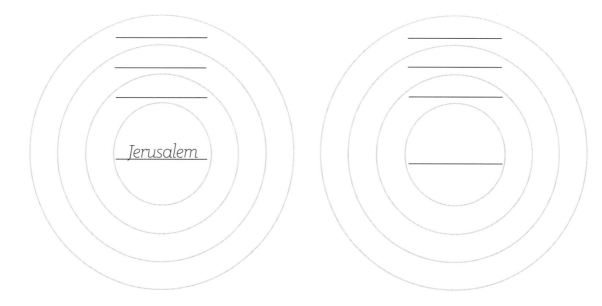

The principle of Jesus' instructions about witnessing is still the same.

In the drawing on the right on page 150, record the name of your town or city in the innermost circle.

Record the name of your state in the next circle and the name of your country in the next.

In the outermost circle, record the same words you recorded in the outermost circle on the left.

Do you agree that this should be your widest area of witnessing?

■ **Read John 15:26-27.**

Based on Acts 1:8 and John 15:26-27, what's the one most important factor required to become a witness for Christ?

Now read Acts 2:13-18 and Ephesians 5:18. What comparison is made in both of these passages?

Both Ephesians 5:18 and Acts 2:13-18 compare drinking wine to being filled with the Holy Spirit. Now read the whole story in Acts 2:1-18. What was the essential ingredient in the witness of these Christians?

Did you respond that the filling of the Holy Spirit was the essential ingredient?

Carefully read the following two statements. Recall Acts 2:1-18 and check the correct statement.

☐ The Holy Spirit simply gave those people a new inner experience and didn't expect them to verbalize it. Bearing a silent witness was enough.

☐ The first act of the Holy Spirit, after filling these people, was to make it possible for them to speak their witness to unbelievers so that every person would hear about Christ.

The right answer was easy, wasn't it? But look! The spectators in Acts 2 thought the Spirit-filled believers were drunk. Peter had to explain that they were full of God's Spirit, not wine.

When people are filled with wine (or any other alcoholic beverage), it takes control of them. They lose all restraint and inhibitions. They say things they probably never would have said otherwise, and they willingly fall to desires of the old nature. Paul said Christians shouldn't let this happen to them. Instead, they need to be so filled with the Holy Spirit that they release the fears and inhibitions that keep them from living and speaking their faith. They're out of control because they're being controlled by the new nature, who's the indwelling Christ.

The greatest hypocrite in the world is someone who says, "I don't have to talk to others about Christ; if they observe my actions, they'll know I'm a Christian." Good old ego! How it loves to protect itself against exposure! But when self is no longer king and Christ reigns, you'll speak about Him.

"But," you may object, "what in my life would be important to an unbeliever?" The important thing is that you've already passed from death to life. Christ's Spirit already lives in you and constantly fills you on request. Remember:

A witness is one who gives evidence. You have much to give evidence about because Christ is living through you.

Your five friends who are open to your sharing are curious about the added ingredient in your life. Don't be afraid. Tomorrow you'll prepare a witnessing testimony. Determine now to share with it with your lost friends.

Record the names of the people you know who are open to your sharing Christ. Decide on a time within the next seven days when you'll share with each one. Beside each name, add the time you've decided to do share.

Name   Time

1. _____   _____

2. _____   _____

3. _____   _____

4. _____   _____

5. _____   _____

End your quiet time by praying for those five friends.

DAY 5

Sharing Your Faith

Read Romans 1:16; Acts 22:1-15; 26:9-20; Matthew 9:10-13; 1 Corinthians 9:19-23.

Do you remember from yesterday's study that when you witness, you're giving evidence? But what's the evidence you're able to present to your lost friends?

You have the evidence of a changed life—of the indwelling Christ, controlling all. You need to verbalize that witness, to tell people who Christ is, what He has done for you, and how much He means to you.

The apostle Paul knew how to verbalize his witness, and he did so at every opportunity to everyone who would listen. Read aloud these words that Paul once wrote:

> I am not ashamed of the gospel, because it is the power
> of God for salvation to everyone who believes.
> **ROMANS 1:16**

Can you honestly make the same statement Paul made? Why or why not?

Scripture records at least two occasions when Paul verbalized his witness, in Acts 22:1-15 and in Acts 26:9-20. In each case the evidence Paul gave was his own conversion experience. In both instances he mentioned four facts about that experience.

■ **Read Acts 22:1-15; 26:9-20.**

Now examine the chart on this page. The four points Paul made are listed and numbered in order on the chart. In the column for each passage, list the verses that contain each point in what Paul said about his conversion. Answers are provided at the end of today's study.

	Acts 22	Acts 26
1. Paul hadn't always followed Christ.	*Verses 3-5*	*Verses 9-12*
2. God began to deal with Paul's rebellion.		
3. Paul received Christ as his Lord.		
4. Paul's new life was centered on Christ's purposes.		

You'll be amazed to discover how few unbelievers have ever heard a Christian share the kind of witness Paul shared in his testimony. Every conversion experience is different from all others. Therefore, your own testimony of the way you came to know Christ is personal and individual. It gives evidence that no one but you can give. No one else will ever duplicate it.

Although your conversion experience is unique, it can probably be outlined in much the same way that Paul outlined his. In fact, the outline should be familiar to you if you're studying *Survival Kit* in a group. You've already used it to begin developing your testimony.

Did you see the similarity between Paul's outline and the outline you used in your group to develop your testimony?

At the end of your quiet time yesterday, I asked you to commit to definite times you'll witness to the five people who are open to listen to you. Twenty-four hours have passed since you made that commitment. Have you taken time to contact them and make appointments?

SURVIVAL KIT

If you have, good for you! If you haven't, do so now before finishing your quiet time. Make those contacts, simply asking them to give you thirty minutes so that you can tell them about the most wonderful, exciting thing that ever happened to you in your life. Then return to finish your quiet time.

Use the following lines to write your testimony in brief, concise, understandable sentences. If you're studying with a group and have already worked on your testimony, revise and refine it one more time.

1. My life and attitudes before I became a Christian:

2. How I realized God was speaking to me:

3. How I became a Christian:

4. What being a Christian means to me:

Recall the time when you became a Christian. A big part of your decision to trust Christ was the influence other people had on you, right? There's no substitute for the personal touch in bringing lost people to Christ.

■ **Read Matthew 9:10-11.**

What criticism did people make of Jesus?

Why do you suppose Jesus risked criticism by having personal contact with people whom others considered unacceptable? Read Matthew 9:12-13 before you answer.

Jesus came to call sinners to repentance. He had mercy or compassion on those who were spiritually sick.

SURVIVAL KIT

■ **Read what the apostle Paul wrote in 1 Corinthians 9:19-21.**

Which of the following statements expresses what Paul meant?

☐ "It doesn't matter to me whom I associate with."
☐ "I agree with whomever I happen to be with at the time."
☐ "I deliberately cultivate the friendship of all sorts of people so that they'll have enough confidence in me to hear my witness."

The last statement summarizes Paul's approach to making friends. Why did Paul feel such an approach was necessary? Read 1 Corinthians 9:22-23 before you answer.

Paul knew not everyone whose friendship he cultivated would accept Christ, but he cultivated friendships with all people in the hope that he would be able to reach as many as possible.

Acts doesn't record a single instance when a person came to know Christ without the aid of a Christian.

Look again at your right hand. Those five people are open to your sharing with them. Determine now that you'll share your testimony with them. This is more than just spending time. You must invest genuine, caring interest in them. You're the riverbed through whom Christ's love can flow to them. As you share your witness with them, they'll see Christ in your words, your life, and your thoughts. They won't be able to escape the impact of Christ, who dwells in you.

Answers to the activity on page 155:
Acts 22: 1. Verses 3-5 2.Verses 6-9 3. Verses 10-13 4.Verses 14-15
Acts 26: 1. Verses 9-12 2. Verses 13-18 3. Verse 19 4. Verses 19-20

REVIEW THIS WEEK'S STUDY

This week you saw the need for effective evangelism in the life of a believer. You studied a plan to help you be committed and intentional in reaching lost friends.

Record the names of the ten people you prayed for this week. Also record a short prayer asking God to draw them to Him.

Friends who refuse to let me share Christ with them:

1. _____

2. _____

3. _____

4. _____

5. _____

Friends who are open to my sharing Christ:

1. _____

2. _____

3. _____

4. _____

5. _____

As you continue walking with Jesus, when will you commit to intentionally pause and pray for these people?

With whom might you replace these names as some of them come to know the Lord?

Spend a few moments thanking God for the ways He has used this study to shape your new life in Christ.

LEADER GUIDE

Prepare to Lead

Each session in the leader guide is designed to be cut out so that you, the leader, can refer to this front-and-back page as you lead the group session. Work through each week's personal studies before studying the corresponding session in the leader guide. Prepare for each group session with prayer, asking the Holy Spirit to work through you.

Minimize Distractions

Do everything in your ability to help people focus on what's most important: connecting with God, with the Bible, and with one another. Create a comfortable environment.

Encourage Discussion

Encourage everyone to ask questions, share responses, or read aloud.

Don't rush through the session. People often need time to think about their responses or to gain courage to share what God is stirring in their hearts.

Affirm and follow up on input from members. Point out something true or helpful in a response instead of just moving on. Ask how other people have experienced similar things or how a truth has shaped their understanding of God and Scripture.

Keep God and His Word central. Trust Scripture to be the authority and God's Spirit to work in people's lives. You can't change anyone, but God can. Continually point people to the Word and to active steps of faith.

SURVIVAL KIT

GROUP ORIENTATION SESSION

The orientation session is a brief meeting to give members their copies of *Survival Kit,* to explain the purpose of the study, and to outline what they'll be expected to do. This session must be conducted at least one week before the group foundation session so that members will be able to complete the foundation week in their books in advance. If possible, schedule this session at the same time and place as the regular sessions. However, the session may be conducted at any time and place and can last only as long as necessary to cover the agenda.

Preparing to Lead the Session

1. Contact all people expected to be in the group. Give information about time and place and confirm their plans to attend.
2. Provide copies of *Survival Kit* for all people you expect to attend. Have extra copies on hand for members you hadn't anticipated.
3. Prepare a testimony-outline poster with the following points.
   - My Life and Attitudes before I Became a Christian
   - How I Realized God Was Speaking to Me
   - How I Became a Christian
   - What Being a Christian Means to Me

4. Trim sheets of paper to the same size as *Survival Kit.* Prepare more sheets than there are members in the group.
5. Prepare your own testimony, using the testimony outline.
6. Arrange the room informally so that members will be comfortable and can see one another.
7. Arrange for light refreshments.
8. Prepare registration cards on which members can record their names, addresses, phone numbers, and email addresses.
9. Provide pencils, felt-tip markers, newsprint, and materials for making name tags.

Leading the Session

1. Serve refreshments to members as they arrive and ask them to prepare name tags and complete registration cards.
2. Introduce yourself, state how long you've been a Christian, and briefly share the reason you're leading this study.

3. Ask members to introduce themselves, tell how long they've been Christians, and state reasons they're completing this study.

4. Distribute copies of *Survival Kit*.

5. Share the personal testimony you prepared. Then display the personal-testimony poster. Distribute the sheets of paper you prepared. Ask members to copy the outline and place it inside the cover of their *Survival Kit*.

6. Direct members to read the first paragraph in the introduction to *Survival Kit*.

7. Ask a member to read John 17. Then lead the group to work together to complete the related activity on page 5. Call special attention to the paragraph that follows the activity (p. 6).

8. Say something like "Whether your Christian life began one week ago or many years ago, Satan is hard at work trying to defeat you. This study will help you get a better grip on how to be a survivor in the Christian life." Then use the material under "Charting Your Course for Survival" to overview the six-week study.

9. Explain the importance of a daily quiet time. State that members should use the daily studies in *Survival Kit* for their quiet times while they're participating in the study.

10. Be sure members understand the following expectations.
    - Members should make every possible effort to attend all group sessions. They should immediately contact you about makeup work for any session missed.
    - Members should complete each day's reading and activities in *Survival Kit*.
    - Members should memorize the assigned Scriptures each week. Call attention to the Scripture-memory cards at the back of the book and suggest ways to use them.

11. Explain that during the next six weeks, group members should be committed to one another as well as to the study. Lead members to form a covenant with one another. Let them suggest what should be included in the covenant, such as doing daily work in *Survival Kit*, helping one another, asking for help, sharing concerns, requesting prayer, and attending all sessions. When the group has agreed on the points to be included, fasten a sheet of newsprint to the wall and ask members to help you organize and compose the covenant. Explain that each person will receive a copy of the covenant at the group foundation session and that all members will sign one another's covenants.

12. Be certain members know the date, time, and place for the group foundation session. Express your understanding that after learning the course expectations, some attendees may want to postpone their participation in the study until a later date.

13. Explain that members are to complete the daily reading and activities in the foundation week before the next group session. Stress the importance of completing the assignments daily and at a time set aside just for that purpose. Also ask them to write a first draft of their testimony, using the outline you've given them.

14. Share concerns and close with prayer.

GROUP FOUNDATION SESSION

FOUNDATION WEEK
The Indwelling Christ, Controlling All

SESSION GOAL. During this session members will discuss problems and joys they experienced in establishing a quiet time, and they'll discuss differences a daily quiet time has produced in their lives this week.

Preparing to Lead the Session

1. Soon after the group orientation session, contact all members who registered and discuss the work they're to do daily before the group foundation session. Affirm any who don't plan to continue the study at this time and encourage them to do so as soon as possible.
2. Prepare copies of a membership list for all members, including names, addresses, phone numbers, and email addresses.
3. Prepare copies of the group covenant, leaving the bottom half of the page blank for signatures. If possible, trim the covenants so that they're the same size as *Survival Kit*.
4. Have newsprint, a felt-tip marker, tape, and pencils available.
5. Display the testimony-outline poster.

Leading the Session

1. Ask: "How are you progressing in learning to locate references in your Bibles?" Allow time for responses. Then ask members to practice locating a passage together. Have them locate the table of contents in the front of their Bibles to find the page on which 2 Corinthians begins. Then have them turn to 2 Corinthians 5:17.
2. Ask one person to read the passage while others follow in their Bibles. Ask: "Who has a translation that states this verse differently? How is it different?" Allow time for responses.
3. Ask: "What characteristics or behaviors have been new or different about you this week because of your work in *Survival Kit*?" Allow time for responses. Ask a volunteer to pray, thanking God for the difference He makes in the lives of Christians.
4. Call attention to the testimony-outline poster and ask members to take turns reading their testimonies to the group. Be encouraging and supportive. Explain that the purpose of this exercise is to help members gain confidence in giving their testimonies and to help them make their testimonies as clear and understandable as possible.
5. Ask members to rewrite their testimonies before the next group session to make them more understandable.

6. Distribute copies of the group covenant. After the group reads the covenant together aloud, ask each member to sign every member's covenant. After all covenants have been signed by all members, ask members to place their copies inside the front cover of their *Survival Kit*.

7. Ask members to describe how they've used this week's Scripture-memory card. Then ask them to repeat the verse to one another in pairs. Praise members for memorizing the assignment and encourage them to continue their good work.

8. Sketch a large hand on a dry-erase board or on a piece of newsprint. Ask members to recall what should be written on the palm (p. 6). Write the correct response on the palm.

9. Emphasize the importance of a quiet time for every growing Christian. Draw attention to the guidelines for a quiet time in day 1 of the foundation week (p. 15). Ask: "Which of these guidelines is giving you the most difficulty?" Be understanding and supportive, not judgmental. Ask members to share with one another ways to deal with their difficulties in having a quiet time. If no one mentions it, bring up the princple "Take time to let Christ speak to you." Explain that meditating on Scripture is one of the best ways to allow God to speak to you. Point out the suggested questions to guide meditation near the end of day 1 in the foundation week (p. 17). Encourage members to try harder during the coming week to let Christ speak to them and to be prepared next week to describe doing so.

10. Ask: "What did you discover this past week as you studied your Bible?" Allow time for responses.

11. Ask: "How did Christ's being in control of your life affect decisions you made this week?" Allow time for discussion.

12. Help members see that Satan doesn't come as a horrible monster who's easy to recognize and reject. He comes in the most beautiful, attractive form possible to deceive us. Often the options he offers are appealing but not the best—not what God wishes for us.

13. Call attention to the course map in the introduction (p. 11) and point out what the group has studied this week. Use the description of week 1 to preview the study for the coming week. Reemphasize the importance of doing work daily and of having a quiet time each day. Make these assignments to be completed before the next group session: (1) Complete the reading and activities in week 1. (2) Memorize the assigned memory verse. (3) Look for a discovery in Bible study and meditation. (4) Rewrite personal testimonies for more clarity and simplicity. (5) Memorize personal testimonies. (6) Be prepared to report on what came to their minds before they became Christians when they heard the words *denomination, church, baptism,* and *holy.*

14. Distribute the membership list. Tell members that it will enable them to contact one another and will serve as a prayer chain. Explain that early in the week, you'll call the first person on the list to talk briefly about the study and to share prayer concerns. That person will then call the next person and so on through the entire list. The last person should call you to confirm that the contact chain has been completed.

15. Ask members to share praises and prayer concerns. Then ask a volunteer to lead the group in prayer, remembering the concerns that have been shared and asking God to bless the work of the group and the fellowship among members during the study.

GROUP SESSION 1

WEEK 1
One Body: Its Life and Service

SESSION GOAL. At the end of this session, group members will be able to explain the sense in which the church is a body and the sense in which it's a building. They will be able to explain the purpose of spiritual gifts and to identify at least one gift they have. They will also be able to state why the body needs each member and why each member needs the body.

Preparing to Lead the Session

1. Begin the prayer chain no later than two days after the previous group session. If you haven't received confirmation that it's been completed within three days, locate the break in the chain and restart it at that point.
2. Prepare a six-inch square of aluminum foil for each person in the group.
3. Provide a sheet of colored construction paper and a pair of scissors for each member.

Leading the Session

1. Express gratitude for the work members are doing. Then ask for praises and concerns they want to share. After a brief sharing period, lead a prayer of thanksgiving and petition.
2. Ask members to look at the course map in the introduction as you preview this session.
3. Direct members to work in pairs (no spouses together) to (1) repeat the Scripture-memory assignment, (2) share from memory their rewritten testimonies, and (3) discuss any activities in week 1 with which they had difficulty during the previous week.
4. Reassemble the group and answer any questions that arose during the work completed in pairs.
5. Ask and discuss: "During your quiet time are you finding it easy or difficult to allow God to speak to you? What difficulties are you experiencing? How are you addressing those difficulties?" Ask volunteers to share what God communicated to them as they meditated on Scripture during the past week.
6. Ask members to share what their responses were before they were Christians to the words *denomination, church, baptism,* and *holy.* Allow time for discussion and questions. Be sure members understand these terms correctly.
7. Ask and discuss: How would you define *lone-ranger Christian?*

8. Distribute sheets of construction paper and scissors. Ask each member to cut out one piece that resembles either a head, an arm, a hand, a torso, a leg, or a foot and to keep the chosen body part a secret. After all body parts have been cut out, collect and give them all to one member. Ask that member to use all the parts to make one body. Point out the incompleteness of the body in the final result.

9. Use the previous activity to teach that God didn't make His church this way. Ask the group to repeat the memory verse for this week and to discuss what it says about the way God puts together His church, the body of Christ. Emphasize that each part is a gift and that the gift fits the church's needs. All of the gifts are united in the body and are used in the body with love.

10. Ask members to share any new or different ideas they learned about spiritual gifts during the previous week.

11. Distribute sheets of aluminum foil to members and ask each person to make a symbol of a spiritual gift they possess. Examples: a coin for giving, a book for knowledge, a towel for service. Any members who have difficulty deciding on a symbol may simply make a box or a bowl to represent a container for the gift.

12. After members have explained their symbols, collect them all. Ask members to give their first reactions as you gently roll all the symbols into a ball. Try to communicate by the way you do so that what you're doing is constructive, not destructive.

13. If members don't begin to respond immediately, say: "Come on now! What are you feeling and thinking?" Someone may blurt out, "You destroyed my gift." Someone else may say, "You messed up my gift." Lead group members to see that the ball is the church. The gifts make up the church but don't stand out alone. Only as a part of the ball (the body, the church) do they have meaning. God gives gifts to individuals to be used in the church to minister to one another's needs and to do the work of Christ.

14. Ask the group to suggest ways they can use their gifts to serve one another in the church and to help the church carry out the work of Christ. Write responses on a dry-erase board or on newsprint fastened to the wall.

15. Say: "Most of our study this week was about the sense in which the church is a body. But we also studied another way Scripture describes the church. How would you describe the sense in which the church is a building?" Allow time for responses and discussion.

16. Remind members to complete the reading and activities in week 2 and to memorize the assigned memory verse before the next group session.

17. Ask each person to bring one piece of fruit to the next group session.

18. Ask members to join hands and listen quietly as you read all stanzas of the hymn "Blest Be the Tie." Then lead a benediction thanking God for the blessing of oneness in the body.

WEEK 2
Two Natures: Old and New

SESSION GOAL. During this session members will identify good fruit that Christ's control is producing in their lives, and they will identify ways to give Christ more complete control during the coming week.

Preparing to Lead the Session

1. Initiate the prayer chain as you did last week. In addition, remind the first caller to pass on the reminder to bring a piece of fruit to the group session.
2. Bring several pieces of fruit for any members who forget.
3. Bring a bowl or basket large enough to hold all the fruit members bring.
4. Provide index cards.

Leading the Session

1. Begin with a sharing and prayer time.
2. Copy the outline of the hand drawing on a dry-erase board or on newsprint and ask members to recall what should be written on the palm, thumb, and index finger. Label the palm and fingers as members respond.
3. Ask members to look at the course map in the introduction. Call attention to the topic for this week and preview this session.
4. Remark that Galatians 5:17 states the reality of the conflict between the two natures. Ask a member to read the verse.
5. Ask members if they can recall the way the Bible describes the inner conflict. Allow time for responses and discussion. Then ask two members to read Romans 7:14-24 from two different modern translations. Compare responses to that passage.
6. State: "The two natures have opposite purposes." Ask members to identify and discuss those purposes.
7. Show the bowl or basket you brought and say: "Let this vessel represent you before you became a Christian. Which nature did you contain?" Distribute index cards to members and ask them to read Galatians 5:19-21 to identify the fruit of the old nature. As each fruit is identified, ask a member to write it on an index card and to place it in the container.

8. Then ask: "But what happened when you became a Christian?" (Your old nature lost its power to produce fruit in you, and your new nature began producing its own fruit.) After members respond and discuss, remove the cards from the basket and give them back to members.

9. Say: "We're going to let the fruit you brought represent the fruit of the new nature. Galatians 5:22-23 identifies the fruit of the new nature." Ask members to place their fruit in the basket while one person reads the passage.

10. Instruct members who received index cards to begin removing pieces of fruit and replacing them with the cards they're holding. Ask: "What's happening?" (The old nature is bearing fruit again in the life of the Christian.)

11. Ask: "How did the new fruit get in?" (The Christian put it in.) "How did the old fruit get back in? Was it because the devil made you do it? Was it because what will be will be?" (No, the Christian let it in.)

12. Write *controller* and *container* on the dry-erase board or on newsprint and lead members to discuss what they learned from their study about the significance of the words.

13. Lead members to review the work they did in week 2, day 5. Guide them to see that containing the right fruit doesn't result from reforming the old nature but from surrendering control to Christ.

14. Ask volunteers to share areas in which they have difficulty surrendering full control to Christ.

15. Lead a closing prayer, remembering the struggles members have shared.

16. Remind members to complete the reading and activities in week 3 and to memorize the assigned memory verse before the next group session.

17. Ask members to bring baby pictures of themselves or another family member to the next group session.

WEEK 3
Three Aspects of Salvation: Beginning, Process, and Completion

SESSION GOAL. At the end of this session, group members should be able to distinguish among salvation past, salvation present, and salvation future. They should also be able to define each term in their own words.

Preparing to Lead the Session

1. Initiate the prayer chain as you did last week. In addition, remind members to bring baby pictures of themselves or of another family member.
2. Collect sheets of newsprint, tape, and a felt-tip marker.
3. Bring a few seeds capable of producing a large plant.

Leading the Session

1. Begin with sharing and prayer concerns. Ask one member to read Philippians 1:3-11 and another to lead in prayer.
2. Reproduce the outline of the hand drawing on a dry-erase board or on newsprint and ask members to recall what should be written on the palm and first three fingers. Label the palm and fingers as members respond.
3. Ask members to look at the course map in the introduction. Call attention to the topic for this week and preview this session.
4. Use Scriptures from this week's activities in *Survival Kit* to lead a Bible drill.
5. Point out that the Scriptures members searched for illustrate the three aspects of salvation. Attach three sheets of newsprint to the wall and ask members to recall what the three aspects are. As members respond, write one aspect at the top of each sheet of newsprint.
6. Ask members to identify salvation past, present, and future in 1 Peter 1:3-9,13.
7. Direct members to work in pairs to check their recall of this week's Scripture-memory assignment. Then ask and discuss: "What does Philippians 1:6 say about the three aspects of salvation?"
8. Ask: "What are some things that can be canceled or undone?" Examples: a bow or knot can be untied, a subscription can be canceled, and a date can be broken.

9. Ask: "What are some things that can't be canceled or undone?" Examples: a gun can't be unshot, a plant can't be unsprouted, and a baby can't be unborn. Then point out that being born again is something that can't be canceled or undone.

10. Lead the group to compose a one-sentence definition of *salvation past*. Write the sentence on the first sheet of newsprint.

11. Point out the seeds you brought. Then ask members to describe the plant one seed will produce.

12. Allow time for members to show their baby pictures and to tell their approximate birth weight. Ask and discuss: "What has happened to your size and appearance since that picture was taken? What if you still looked exactly like the person in the picture after all these years? What would you say about a Christian who continues year after year to look spiritually the same as she did when she was born again? What should happen to a person's spiritual size and appearance with passing months and years?"

13. Point out that the change in a person's spiritual size and appearance is what we call salvation present.

14. Be certain members understand the meaning of the word *incarnation*. State that Scripture teaches that Jesus is our great High Priest who intercedes for us. Then ask and discuss: "How did Jesus' incarnation help prepare Him for His role as our High Priest?"

15. Direct members to locate Hebrews 4:14-16 in their Bibles and ask them to read the verses from several different translations. Then ask one or two members to share testimonies of times when they called on Jesus for help during the past week.

16. Read aloud 1 Corinthians 10:13 and ask: "What does this verse tell us about the difficulties we face in our Christian lives?" After members have responded, pause to pray, thanking God for providing His grace. Specifically pray about the testimonies that have been shared.

17. Review material at the beginning of week 3, day 4 to be sure members understand the meaning of being filled with the Spirit. Being filled isn't a matter of capacity (how much of the Spirit we have) but of possession (how much the Spirit has us).

18. Guide the group to compose a one-sentence definition of *salvation present*. Record it on the newsprint.

19. Ask and discuss: "In what sense will our salvation be incomplete until sometime in the future?"

20. Guide members to compose a one-sentence definition of *salvation future* and write it on the newsprint.

21. Remind members to complete the reading and activities in week 4 and to memorize the assigned memory verses before the next group session.

22. Close in prayer, thanking God for the security of your eternal salvation that Jesus provided on the cross.

GROUP SESSION 4

WEEK 4
Four Sources of Authority: Inadequate and Adequate

SESSION GOAL. At the end of this session, members will be able to explain (1) why tradition, experiences, and intellect are inadequate standards for determining truth; (2) how these three sources relate to Scripture in determining truth; and (3) why the Bible is the one true authority for the Christian life.

Preparing to Lead the Session

1. Initiate the prayer chain as you have each week.
2. Enlist a member to tell this story. A newly married couple was preparing to cook a whole ham together. The wife cut off the shank, or hock, and threw it away. When her husband asked why she cut off and threw away good meat, she replied, "Well, Mother always did." The next time they were at her mother's, he asked the mother why she had always cut off the ham hock and thrown it away. The mother replied, "Grandma always did." When Grandma came into the room, the young man asked her, "Why did you always cut off the ham hock and throw it away?" Grandma responded, "Because my pan was too small to hold the whole ham!"
3. Enlist a member to tell this story. Four blind men were examining an elephant. One man felt the trunk and said, "This animal is round and long and has an open mouth at one end." The second man, feeling the elephant's leg, said, "Oh no! This animal is like a tree." The third man grasped the tail and said, "No, you're both wrong. It's small like a snake and has hair at the end." The final man, who was sitting on the elephant, said, "You guys don't know what you're talking about. This animal is as big and round as a blimp."
4. Gather copies of *The Baptist Faith and Message* tract. If possible, provide a copy for each member.

Leading the Session

1. Begin with sharing and prayer concerns. Lead in prayer.
2. Draw the outline of the hand drawing on a dry-erase board or on newsprint and ask members to recall what should be written on the palm and first four fingers. Label the palm and fingers as members respond.

3. Ask members to look at the course map in the introduction. Call attention to the topic for this week and preview this session. Then ask and discuss: "If you were going to sum up this week's study in one sentence, what would you say?"

4. Call on the member enlisted to tell the story of Grandma's ham hock. After the story ask members to suggest morals from the story that can be applied to blindly following church traditions. Examples: (1) Traditions may have begun for reasons that no longer apply. (2) Traditions regularly need to be evaluated in light of present resources and needs. (3) Traditions have little value in themselves but in the way they meet a need.

5. Call on the member enlisted to tell the story of the blind men and the elephant. Then ask members to discuss the danger of using feelings and experiences to validate religious ideas. (Faith and religious experience extend beyond what our feelings and experiences can tell us. Relying on feelings and experiences has defined limits. Feelings and experiences aren't always a true reflection of reality. God is with us regardless of how high or low our feelings may be.)

6. Ask volunteers to describe times when they were misled by their feelings, senses, or perception of reality.

7. Ask members to discuss their response to this statement: "Believe only what you can see, prove, or understand." Lead them to see that intellect ultimately rests on faith. We can't see and document emotion, thoughts, ideas, love, electricity, atoms, and so on. We live by and accept much that we can't see or ultimately can't prove.

8. Direct the group to turn to the chart they completed in week 4, day 1. Identify the important distinctions in the definitions on the chart. Three sources of authority come from sources we structure or determine. The distinctive Christian stance is that God reveals truth by His own initiative, choice, and love. Ask: "Which of your Scripture-memory assignments for this week applies to these three sources?" (1 Corinthians 2:14). Ask members to form pairs to check their recall of the verse.

9. Ask: "Which Scripture-memory assignment for this week tells the one true source of authority for Christians?" (2 Timothy 3:16). Ask the same pairs to check their recall of this verse.

10. Read aloud the statement on the Scriptures from page 7 in the tract *The Baptist Faith and Message.* If enough copies are available, give one to each member. Then ask members to recall from their study and discuss (1) reasons the Bible is the one true source of authority for Christians and (2) how the other sources of authority relate to the Bible in determining truth.

11. Remind members to complete the reading and activities in week 5 and to memorize the assigned memory verses before the next group session. Inform them that day 5 in their daily study this week will ask them to share their testimonies with at least one person before the next group session.

12. Close with prayer, thanking God for His authoritative, all-sufficient Word.

WEEK 5

The Five-and-Five Principle: Reaching Others through Prayer and Witnessing

SESSION GOAL. During this session members will practice sharing their testimonies, discuss plans for sharing their testimonies, and review what they've learned during their study of *Survival Kit*.

Preparing to Lead the Session

1. Initiate the prayer chain as you've done each week. Ask each person to pass along the reminder that week 5, day 5 calls for them to share their testimonies with at least one person before group session 5.
2. Have blank sheets of paper available for the session.

Leading the Session

1. Begin with sharing and prayer concerns. Lead in prayer.
2. Ask members to look at the course map in the introduction. Call attention to the topic for this week and preview this session.
3. Ask volunteers to share any witnessing experiences they've had with someone who wasn't open to a testimony. Ask them to describe the experience, how it made them feel, and what they did after their witness was rejected. Allow ample time for sharing and discussion. Be as sensitive and supportive as possible. Don't hesitate to pause and pray if a member seems discouraged or burdened.
4. Ask and discuss: "How did you respond to the idea that you can win people without actually witnessing to them?"
5. Ask and discuss: "Does the fact that we can begin winning people without witnessing to them mean witnessing isn't necessary?" (Of course not! We should seek and witness to people who'll listen to us, and we should pray for those who won't.)
6. Ask members to describe the way they felt as they prayed for people who aren't open to hearing their witness.
7. Divide members into twos or threes and assign this two-step activity to each group: (1) Ask members to share one name from their lists of persons who won't hear their

witness; why they can't witness to that person; and ways they're asking, seeking, and knocking in prayer for that person. (2) After individual sharing is complete, pray together for each person mentioned in the sharing.

8. Reassemble the group and ask members to share their testimonies from week 5, day 5 and to tell about their experiences sharing those testimonies with a lost person.

9. Spend the remaining time bringing closure to the study. Express appreciation for members' hard work and for the friendships that have been formed.

10. Join hands in a circle and lead a final prayer of thanksgiving and praise for the difference Jesus has made in members' lives.

ONE-TO-ONE DISCIPLESHIP GUIDE

A Note to the Discipler

This one-to-one discipleship guide is primarily intended for use in guiding a new Christian through an individual study of *Survival Kit*. Before attempting to serve as a discipler or guide to a new Christian, you should have completed *Survival Kit* and should be thoroughly familiar with its content and the process. You also should have memorized all of the Scripture-memory verses.

This guide gives directions for a one-to-one orientation session, a one-to-one foundation session, and five one-to-one sessions for guiding your new friend through a one-to-one study of *Survival Kit*. In general, the one-to-one sessions will follow this plan.

Scripture Memory

Beginning with the one-to-one foundation session, you'll have Scripture-memory verses to review each week. At each session you and your friend should do the following.

1. Quote all verses memorized, including references.
2. Share special meanings the verse or verses have had in your lives this week.
3. Review the verse or verses for the next week.

Questions

You'll use Scripture passages to give encouragement and assurance about doubts and questions related to the study for that week. The questions your friend will have each week will be unique. This guide will suggest several questions. Use the ones you think will be helpful or will deepen your friend's understanding of the study material.

Jesus' Example

You'll examine Scripture passages to learn how Jesus taught and lived the truth you and your friend have studied during the previous week.

Assignments

You'll review work to be done during the coming week.

A Note to the Disciple

With this one-to-one discipleship guide you'll journey through an individual study of *Survival Kit* with someone who has completed the study before. Your discipler will be familiar with the content and the process of this study.

This guide gives directions for a one-to-one orientation session, a one-to-one foundation session, and five one-to-one sessions for walking through a one-to-one study of *Survival Kit* with your discipler. In general, the one-to-one sessions will follow this plan.

Scripture Memory

Beginning with the one-to-one foundation session, you'll have Scripture-memory verses to review each week. At each session you and your discipler should do the following.

1. Recite all verses memorized, including references.
2. Share special meanings the verse or verses have had in your lives this week.
3. Review the verse or verses for the next week.

Questions

Your discipler will use Scripture passages to give you encouragement and assurance about doubts and questions you might have about the study for that week. This guide will suggest several questions that you and your discipler can discuss in addition to your own unique questions.

Jesus' Example

You and your discipler will examine Scripture passages to learn how Jesus taught and lived the truth you have studied during the previous week.

Assignments

You'll review work to be done during the coming week.

ONE-TO-ONE
ORIENTATION SESSION

As soon as possible, have a one-to-one orientation session with the person you'll counsel. Do the following in this session.

1. Select a convenient time to meet each week for the next six weeks. Allow a minimum of forty-five minutes for each one-to-one session.
2. Share what Christ has done in your life.
3. Present a copy of *Survival Kit* to the person you'll be counseling and review the introduction to the book. Explain the meaning of *survival* as it's used in this study. Be sure your friend understands he's in no danger of losing his salvation. Then briefly overview the topics that will be covered in the study by referring to the course map on page 11.
4. Read together the verses on page 178. Point out that Paul's instruction to Timothy summarizes the one-to-one discipling relationship you will have during your study of *Survival Kit*.
5. If your friend doesn't have a study Bible, make arrangements to purchase one before the next session.
6. Point out the Scripture-memory cards at the back of the book. Explain the importance of using these cards and of memorizing the assigned Scripture verse or verses each week.

   - Point out the daily reading and activities. Explain that these daily studies are to nurture a meaningful, devoted, growing Christian life. Encourage the consistent completion of each day's work.
   - Assign the reading and activities in the foundation week for the first week of study. Explain that each daily study will require about twenty minutes.

7. During the week call your friend and encourage her daily study habit. Answer any questions she may have about completing the daily activities. Ask whether she has any special requests and assure her of your prayers.

Paul and Timothy

A Discipling Relationship

You, therefore, my son, be strong in the grace that is in Christ Jesus. What you have heard from me in the presence of many witnesses, commit to faithful men who will be able to teach others also.

2 TIMOTHY 2:1-2

ONE-TO-ONE FOUNDATION SESSION

FOUNDATION WEEK
The Indwelling Christ, Controlling All

Scripture Memory

1. Quote the verse memorized, including the reference.
2. Share special meanings the verse has had in your lives this week.
3. Be patient if the person is having trouble learning to memorize Scripture. Review the guidelines in day 2 of the foundation week.
4. Review the verse for the next week.

Questions

Assurance Checkup

Use 2 Corinthians 5:17 to affirm that we're new creations because we're in Christ. Describe changes Christ has brought about in your life. Pray together, thanking God that Christ has come into your lives. Then discuss any doubts your friend may have about salvation.

Address Questions about the Week's Study

1. *I find it hard to study* Survival Kit *each day.* Daily study is a discipline. Share ways you've benefited from having a personal quiet time. Nothing worthwhile comes without planning for it and devoting time to it.
2. *Is memorizing Scriptures really necessary?* No. You don't have to memorize Scripture to be a Christian. But doing so is a great aid to spiritual growth, and having Scriptures in your memory is a powerful weapon for facing Satan's attacks and temptations.
3. *Does prayer really change anything? Won't God do the right thing whether or not we ask Him?* This question misses the whole point of prayer. Praying is a training ground where God transforms us into Christlikeness, reveals His will to us, and equips us to be channels of His grace and His work.
4. *I'm having difficulty overcoming old habits.* Review day 4 of the foundation week. Discuss the power Christ has (see Matthew 28:18) and the availability of that power to overcome bad habits.

5. *How do I tell my friends what has happened to me?* Ask for a few details about specific friends who need to be told the good news of your friend's salvation. Suggest ways to approach each one.

Jesus' Example

Jesus not only taught the truth but also lived it. Examine the following Scriptures to learn how His life illustrated the truth taught in *Survival Kit* this week.

1. Jesus had a quiet time: Mark 1:35.
2. Jesus memorized the Scriptures: Matthew 4:4,7,10.
3. Jesus prayed about the details of His life: Luke 11:1.
4. Jesus faced every temptation we face: Hebrews 4:15-16.
5. Jesus shared with others the relationship He had with His Father: John 14:6-7.

Assignments

1. Encourage your new friend to continue studying *Survival Kit* daily. Assign the reading and activities in week 1 for next week's one-to-one session. Preview these lessons, which focus on one body, the church.
2. Share the importance of church membership in your life. Encourage your friend to join the fellowship of a local church if he hasn't already done so.
3. Share the way you discovered your spiritual gifts and name people whose gifts have ministered to you in a special way.
4. If you've discussed particular habits or problem areas, agree on a time to pray daily about them.

WEEK 1
One Body: Its Life and Service

Scripture Memory

1. Quote the verse memorized, including the reference.
2. Share special meanings the verse has had in your lives this week.
3. Review the verse for the next week.

Questions

Assurance Checkup

1. Use 1 John 5:11-12 to reassure your friend that we're eternally forgiven and saved in Christ.
2. Use John 10:28 to show that Christ firmly grasps us, assuring us that we'll never perish.
3. Use 1 John 1:9 to show that Christ readily forgives us when we fail.
4. Use Psalm 119:11 to point out that the Scriptures give us help as we turn away from sin.

Address Questions about the Week's Study

These questions relate to the material studied. However, if your friend has greater concerns, put them first. Discuss at least one or two of these questions to reinforce the truths studied this week.

1. *Why did Paul use a human body to describe the church?* Because the church is an organism, not an organization.
2. *After studying* Survival Kit *for five days, what should I do the other two days?* Use these days to prepare for Bible-study and discipleship groups. You may also wish to use part of the time to review your Scripture-memory verses.
3. *Why is fellowship with other Christians important?* Remind your friend that Christians have spiritual gifts that make important contributions to one another's spiritual growth. Review the meaning of the phrase "no lone-ranger Christians."

4. *How can I share my new life with others?* If this question is asked, you may wish to skip ahead to week 5, day 5 and help your friend prepare a one-minute testimony to use now.

5. *How does Christian love differ from non-Christian love?* Non-Christian love is rooted in the character of the person. This love is often based on feelings or on what the person gets in return. Christian love is rooted in the character of God and reveals His character.

6. *Can I use spiritual gifts without divine love?* No. Spiritual gifts are the love of God flowing through you to others.

7. *What does being conformed to the world mean (see Romans 12:1-3)?* Being conformed to this world means living according to the standards, values, and priorities of this world.

8. *What does renewing the mind mean?* Renewing the mind is establishing, confirming, and redirecting your mind toward the priorities and purposes of the Holy Spirit. It's making decisions and carrying out actions that serve the purpose of Christ and that bring glory to God.

9. *How do I discover my unique spiritual gifts?* Review the material in week 1, days 3–4. Encourage your new friend to be patient and to seek God's leadership, along with the counsel and affirmation of other Christians.

Jesus' Example

Use the following Scriptures to show how Jesus' life illustrated the truth taught in *Survival Kit* this week.

1. Jesus meets our spiritual needs: John 2:19-22.
2. Jesus was in constant fellowship with others: Luke 22:11-16.
3. Jesus constantly drew others to the Father: John 4:39-42.
4. Jesus always depended on the Father's power: John 5:19.

Assignments

1. Assign the reading and activities in week 2 for next week's one-to-one session. Preview the material.
2. Pray together and encourage your friend to begin praying aloud with you.
3. Review problems you've discussed and commit to continue praying at a specific time about those problems.
4. Ask whether you can meet with your friend's unsaved friends and relatives.

ONE-TO-ONE SESSION 2

WEEK 2
Two Natures: Old and New

Scripture Memory

1. Quote the verse memorized, including the reference.
2. Share special meanings the verse has had in your lives this week.
3. Review the verse for the next week.

Questions

Assurance Checkup

1. Use Psalm 32:5 to discuss the ready forgiveness that's ours if we deal directly with sin.
2. Confession brings about forgiveness (see 1 John 1:9).
3. Use Psalm 119:105 to discuss the source we have for determining God's will. The Scriptures give us principles for living in every area of life. The Bible is a totally reliable guide to help us discover God's will in any situation.

Address Questions about the Week's Study

1. *Does the old nature change or improve after I become a Christian?* No. Galatians 5:17 describes the constant choice a Christian must make. When we choose to have Christ's nature in us, we have victory. When we choose to have the old nature in us, defeat is certain.
2. *What's the value of resolving to improve?* Not much if your decision is on the level of a New Year's resolution. The old nature is never going to be disciplined into being better than it is. However, if your resolve to improve is the first stage of repentance, it may have value, but it's only the beginning of the process.
3. *Is peace between my two natures possible?* Not in the sense that a truce is declared. However, Romans 8:2 indicates that we can be free from the conflict between the two natures by deliberately, constantly choosing to let Christ reign in our lives.
4. *Does Christ's indwelling presence depend on my obedience?* No. See Galatians 4:6. The fact that you're God's child isn't based on what you do but on the fact that God is your Father (see John 1:12-13).

5. *Why do Christians become defeated or discouraged?* Primarily because we choose to trust ourselves rather than God or because we choose to follow our own will rather than God's will. When we choose to let God's will reign in our lives, defeat and discouragement are ruled out.

Jesus' Example

1. Jesus knew our old nature would require us to forgive one another again and again: Matthew 18:21-22.
2. Jesus knows our danger zones: Matthew 4:1-11.
3. Jesus is praying for us even before we're tempted: Luke 22:31-32.
4. Jesus taught that the consequences of life depend on our foundation: Matthew 7:24-27.
5. Jesus showed His power over the flesh: John 11:43-44.
6. Jesus assures us that His strength is available to us for today: Matthew 6:11,34.

Assignments

1. Assign the reading and activities in week 3 for next week's one-to-one session. Preview the material.
2. Review the course map in the introduction, calling attention to the week titles. Briefly summarize upcoming topics.
3. Pray together. Remember to address areas of conflict between the old and new natures that you've discussed during this session.

ONE-TO-ONE SESSION 3

WEEK 3
Three Aspects of Salvation: Beginning, Process, and Completion

Scripture Memory

1. Quote the verse memorized, including the reference.
2. Emphasize the importance of knowing references as well as Scriptures. Always say the reference before and after you quote the verse.
3. Share special meanings the verse has had in your lives this week.
4. Review the verses for the next week.

Questions
Assurance Checkup

Share Proverbs 3:5-6, focusing on the statement "Do not rely on your own understanding" (v. 5). Discuss the way this statement relates to searching the Bible for answers to our questions. Point out that uncertainty isn't the same as unbelief and that God has an answer for each of our questions. Asking God for answers to uncertainties and questions isn't wrong. Then meditate together on Proverbs 28:13. Focus on the idea that our sins are covered. Confessing and forsaking sin don't earn forgiveness. Rather, God responds to our repentance by forgiving us even though we don't deserve it. God's love isn't a reward for being good. Our sin doesn't change the fact that we're His children.

Address Questions about the Week's Study

1. *Is my salvation incomplete at the present time?* It's complete in the sense that it can't be lost. Freedom from the penalty of sin is complete. Salvation is in process in the sense that, day by day, our risen Lord indwells us to deliver us from the constant power and influence of sin. Salvation won't be finally and ultimately complete until a time in the future when Jesus returns and delivers us from even the presence of sin.

2. *Does the daily aspect of salvation mean I can sin as much as I want to?* Do you want to sin? God's indwelling Son should be taking away the desire to sin. Anything that doesn't glorify Christ becomes less and less enjoyable. First John 2:9-10 underlines this point.

3. *How do I know when I'm filled with the Spirit?* Being filled with the Spirit produces observable results in your life. Galatians 5:22-23 lists nine characteristics of the person who's been filled with the Spirit.

4. *Is being filled with the Spirit a one-time experience?* No. Receiving His presence is a one-time experience that happens the moment you believe. How much you're filled with His power depends on your obedience to Him and your trust in Him. You learned this week that Ephesians 5:18 tells you to be filled continually. God wants to help you grow toward maturity. As you do so, you face different challenges in life for which you need to be filled by His Spirit. As each new challenge appears, He's present to fill that need with Himself.

5. *Where do I get the power to work out my salvation?* Matthew 28:18 tells you that Jesus has all power in heaven and on earth. The One who has all that power lives in you. You don't get the power. You have the One who has all power and authority.

Jesus' Example

1. Jesus assures us of salvation present: Matthew 11:28-30.
2. Jesus gives us a new purpose when He saves us: Luke 5:10-11.
3. Jesus taught that salvation involves growth: John 16:12-15.
4. Jesus frees us from sin's slavery: John 8:31-36.
5. Jesus enables us to trust Him instead of our own resources: John 21:15-19.
6. Jesus understands our lack of understanding about our weaknesses: Matthew 26:33-35.
7. Jesus will raise us up on the last day: John 6:38-40.
8. Jesus expects us to have an unquenchable thirst for Him: John 7:37; Revelation 21:6; 22:17.

Assignments

1. Assign the reading and activities in week 4 for next week's one-to-one session. Preview the material.
2. Stress again the importance of a daily, habitual time for study, meditation, and prayer.
3. Pray together, praising the Lord for recently answered prayers.

WEEK 4
Four Sources of Authority: Inadequate and Adequate

Scripture Memory

1. Quote the verses memorized, including the references.
2. Share special meanings the verses have had in your lives this week.
3. Share experiences you and your friend have had applying the verses to life situations.
4. Review the verses for the next week.

Questions
Assurance Checkup

1. Discuss together Romans 10:17. Why must hearing precede faith? Faith doesn't happen automatically. It's the result of a process. First comes authority: the Word of Christ. Second comes an awareness of the authority: hearing the Word of Christ. Third comes faith: the complete, total trust we place in what we hear and know about Christ from Scripture.
2. Discuss with your friend the meaning of being spiritual. Read Galatians 5:16. Then point out that a person isn't spiritual because of knowledge, intellect, or experiences. Rather, a person is spiritual because of a right relationship with the Holy Spirit. Spirituality is a continual process of life in which we're sensitive to the Holy Spirit.

Address Questions about the Week's Study

1. *Why is my intellect inadequate to make judgments?* Absolute knowledge of right and wrong rests with God. When sin entered the human race, everything was corrupted and fell under its influence, including our intellect. We can't trust our human minds to reason with absolute accuracy what's right and wrong. Only God can reveal that truth to us.
2. *Why do people get caught in cults and follow false leaders?* Because they believe a person, an experience, or a philosophy is the source of truth. Jesus firmly rebuked this deadly trap.

3. *Are all religious traditions dangerous?* No. Many traditions practice within the framework of Scriptures. Traditions become dangerous when we make them more important than the Scriptures, especially when those traditions contradict God's clear teaching. Some traditions may not be wrong as much as they're dated, losing meaning as times or cultures change.

4. *How can I understand the Bible better than I do?* First, continue the lifelong habit of reading Scripture and meditating on it daily. Second, study under the direction of qualified, respected teachers. Third, use good Bible-study tools. These include a study Bible, a Bible dictionary, a concordance, and Bible commentaries.

5. *Can people find God apart from the Bible?* Yes. See Romans 1:20. However, apart from the Bible, people can't find the record of Jesus Christ and the way God has provided salvation for all people through His death and resurrection.

Jesus' Example

1. Jesus stressed the permanent value of Scripture: Matthew 5:17-20.
2. Jesus faulted tradition as an inadequate authority: Matthew 23:1-31.
3. Jesus faulted human experiences as an inadequate source of authority: Mark 8:12; Luke 11:29-32.
4. Jesus faulted intellect alone as an inadequate authority: Matthew 22:23-29.
5. Jesus taught us to search the Scriptures to find Him: John 5:38-40.
6. Jesus said the Holy Spirit would teach us as we study the Scriptures: John 16:13-15.
7. Jesus gave us the Scriptures so that we would believe in Him: John 20:30-31.

Assignments

1. Assign the reading and activities in week 5 for next week's one-to-one session. Preview the material.

2. Point out that 1 Corinthians 11:31 instructs us to examine ourselves as a part of the pattern for our Christian growth. Lead your friend to list personal strengths and weaknesses. Then discuss ways the strengths can be used during the coming week and ways Christ can show His sufficiency in each area of weakness.

3. Discuss with your friend the effects of peer pressure. Share some struggles you've had in this area. Encourage your friend to identify ways to use the Scriptures as authority to deal with peer pressure in the everyday matters of life. Then lead your friend to determine necessary actions for dealing with peer pressure.

4. Pray together, laying before the Lord each weakness and claiming His strength as sufficient for every challenge you face.

WEEK 5
The Five-and-Five Principle: Reaching Others through Prayer and Witnessing

Scripture Memory

1. Quote the verses memorized, including the references.
2. Stress the meaning of the word *everything* in Philippians 4:6. Discuss these questions: What does this verse mean? How do we pray for the lost in the spirit of this verse? How can this verse strengthen us in the daily pressures we face?
3. Share special meanings the verses have had in your lives this week.
4. Discuss the importance of continuing to memorize Scripture after this study is completed.

Questions

Assurance Checkup

Emphasize the assurance your friend can have that Christ will help her win others.

1. Read together Jeremiah 33:3. Point out that we don't need to worry about the future. God knows the future; we can leave it in His hands.
2. Apart from prayer we're powerless to address the unbelief of our friends. Through prayer we're able to bring the lost to salvation.

Address Questions about the Week's Study

1. *In 1 Timothy 2:8 what's meant by praying "without anger or argument"?* Read 1 John 1:6-7. Our prayers reflect our inner spirit. When we try to pray while we have anger toward another person or while we have quarrelsome thoughts, our prayers reflect that spirit. Because group prayer is mentioned in 1 Timothy 2:8, such attitudes could be reflected in our prayers. Such praying causes even more tension. Problems in the fellowship of the church should be resolved so that prayer can be an act of unity and love.
2. *How long will it take for God to answer my prayers?* God knows when the conditions are right for your prayers to be answered. Many times what appears to be a delay in seeing our prayers answered is simply God's preparation time.

3. *What does it mean to pray in Jesus' name?* Prayers made in Jesus' name are prayers that are consistent with His nature, under the leadership of the Holy Spirit, and in accordance with His will.
4. *Why did Jesus tell His disciples to begin witnessing in Jerusalem before going to other areas?* Because He was in Jerusalem when He spoke these words. Jesus was saying that no person was to be bypassed, and His disciples were to begin telling about Him right where they were.
5. *How do I give evidence of the good news to others?* By the way you live, by the words you speak, and by your servant spirit toward unbelievers.

Jesus' Example

1. Jesus prayed that He would be used to redeem the lost: Mark 14:32-36.
2. Jesus taught that we must ask before we can receive: John 16:23.
3. Jesus taught us to serve unbelievers: Matthew 5:40-48.
4. Jesus promised power for witnessing: Acts 1:8.

Closure

1. Discuss with your friend what commitments you'd like to make to each other about your future relationship. Emphasize the possibility of continuing to be prayer and faith-sharing partners.
2. Read 2 Timothy 2:2 and encourage your friend to use *Survival Kit* to help another person, possibly one who has recently become a Christian. Explain that your ministry isn't complete until this step occurs.
3. Share ways this experience has helped you grow as a Christian. Then pray together, thanking and praising God for the hours you've spent together and for the difference that time has made in your lives.

BE INTENTIONAL ABOUT GROWING AS A DISCIPLE.

Disciples Path is a series of six resources founded on Jesus' model of discipleship. It provides an intentional path for transformational discipleship created by experienced disciple makers across the nation. While most small-group studies facilitate transformation through relationship and information, these disciple-making resources do it through the principles of modeling, practicing, and multiplying:

- Leaders model a biblical life.
- Disciples follow and practice from the leader's example.
- Disciples become disciple makers and multiply through Disciples Path.

Learn more at lifeway.com/disciplespath

Lifeway